CHILDREN *Surviving* IN A WORLD OF VIOLENCE

35 LESSONS FOR STUDENTS IN GRADES 5–9

BY CAMMIE MCDANIEL

ILLUSTRATED BY MELINDA FABIAN

copyright © 2000
mar∗co products, inc.

Published by
mar∗co products, inc.
1443 Old York Road
Warminster, PA 18974
1-800-448-2197

All rights reserved including the right of reproduction in whole or in part in any form. The purchaser may reproduce the activity sheets, free and without special permission, for student use for a particular group or class. Reproduction of these materials for distribution to any person other than the purchaser or to an entire school system is forbidden.

Library of Congress Catalog Card Number: 99-69977

ISBN: 1-57543-083-5

Printed in the U.S.A.

CONTENTS

INTRODUCTION 6

HOW TO USE *CHILDREN SURVIVING IN A WORLD OF VIOLENCE* 7

VIOLENCE AND ITS CONSEQUENCES 9
    SESSION 1: WHAT IS VIOLENCE? 10
    SESSION 2: FORMS OF VIOLENCE 14
    SESSION 3: CAUSES OF VIOLENCE 18
    SESSION 4: TELEVISION AND VIOLENCE 22
    SESSION 5: THE IMPACT OF TELEVISION AND MOVIE VIOLENCE 24
    SESSION 6: WHAT IS JUVENILE CRIME? 28
    SESSION 7: BEING A KID ISN'T EASY 32

THE IMPORTANCE OF FAMILY VALUES 37
    SESSION 8: FAMILIES 38
    SESSION 9: FAMILY RULES 42
    SESSION 10: YOU AND YOUR FAMILY 44

ANGER AND WHAT TO DO ABOUT IT 47
    SESSION 11: WHEN ANGER TAKES OVER—WHO'S IN CONTROL? 48
    SESSION 12: MANAGING ANGER 50
    SESSION 13: NEGATIVE BEHAVIORS I NEED TO WORK ON 56
    SESSION 14: ALTERNATIVES TO FIGHTING 60
    SESSION 15: ANGER ALTERNATIVES 64

CONFLICT-RESOLUTION 69
    SESSION 16: WHAT IS CONFLICT? 70
    SESSION 17: CHOICES! CHOICES! CHOICES! 74
    SESSION 18: FIGHT FAIRLY IN CONFLICT SITUATIONS 78

SAFE SURROUNDINGS 81
    SESSION 19: SAFE PLACES AND PEOPLE 82
    SESSION 20: WHAT MAKES A HOME SAFE? 86
    SESSION 21: SAFE NEIGHBORHOODS 90
    SESSION 22: SCHOOL AS A SAFE PLACE 94
    SESSION 23: EVERYONE AND EVERYTHING HAS A RIGHT TO LIVE 98

POTENTIALLY DESTRUCTIVE BEHAVIORS 101
    SESSION 24: BOTTLING UP EMOTIONS 102
    SESSION 25: PREJUDICE 106
    SESSION 26: FEAR 110

CONSTRUCTIVE BEHAVIORS 113
    SESSION 27: POSITIVE FEELINGS 114
    SESSION 28: COMMUNICATING THROUGH BODY LANGUAGE 118
    SESSION 29: GOOD MANNERS LEAD TO GOOD BEHAVIOR 122
    SESSION 30: SETTING GOALS 126
    SESSION 31: SELECTING AND KEEPING FRIENDS 130

SELF-AWARENESS 135
    SESSION 32: SELF-ESTEEM 136
    SESSION 33: I NEED TO IMPROVE 140
    SESSION 34: GOOD SELF-ESTEEM MAKES YOU FEEL GOOD 142
    SESSION 35: I AM A STRONG PERSON 146

GLOSSARY 149

CHILDREN *Surviving* IN A WORLD OF VIOLENCE

INTRODUCTION

Violence is ever-present in today's schools and neighborhoods. Areas which were once considered safe are no longer immune to gang-related incidents, in-school shootings, and other violent behaviors. Educators and social scientists ponder endlessly over the reasons that cause some children to be nonviolent while others act out in ways that are devastating to themselves and unthinkable to others.

Children Surviving in a World of Violence attempts to address possible solutions for these behaviors. It is meant to help teachers, counselors, social workers, and other group leaders overcome many of the obstacles involved in educating children about this important topic. It is also intended to help guide educators through these troubled times. Its purpose is to educate children about violence, regardless of where they live, because none of us is immune to what goes on in the world around us. Crime is no longer restricted to the inner city. Stories about 5- and 6-year-old children bringing guns and other weapons to school, child abuse, school-age children being killed by gangs in cross-fires, and children killing children in school and neighborhood settings are so frequently reported that they are no longer startling. Crime is everywhere. And in order to survive in a world of violence, children must be educated to prevent violence from happening to them and the ones they love. Children need to know how to avoid violence whenever possible and how to handle violence when it is thrust upon them.

In schools today, teachers encounter children who flash gang signs and talk freely about gangs, drugs, and violence. Although it is true that children have always incorporated some violence into their play, the extent of violence seen in school today has progressed from innocent play to frightening reality. Profanity and threats are a part of everyday language and life. Where does it all come from? Children pattern themselves after TV characters, older siblings, and parents. When violent behaviors are seen by children, they unconsciously become a part of their lives. There is a crossover from the streets and homes to the schools.

The most common forms of violence are the daily attacks on individuals' self-esteem and dignity in the forms of verbal abuse and put-downs. Children learn early in life to protect themselves against the outside world, especially a world that attacks them rather than protects them. Researchers are beginning to conclude that abuse and neglect can reset the brain's chemistry and that bad environments can create an epidemic of violence.

Children Surviving in a World of Violence is designed with the understanding that, in these dangerous and troubled times, children need positive adult role-models who are caring and strong, capable of setting limits and boundaries, and capable of enforcing rules of discipline. The lessons focus on:

- safety issues
- life skills
- gangs
- positive preventive measures
- approaches to change.

These lessons are about learning and teaching others positive actions and activities to use in lieu of destructive, negative behaviors.

HOW TO USE
CHILDREN SURVIVING IN A WORLD OF VIOLENCE

The program consists of 35 lessons related to understanding violence and learning how to avoid violent behaviors.

Each lesson includes:

- a leader's guide
- reproducible information and activities for the students.

The target population is students aged 10 to 14, or grades 5 through 9.

ORGANIZING THE PROGRAM

Although the lessons presented in the book are in sequential order, time may prevent you from using each one. If this is the case, present the first four lessons, then select those you feel are most important for your students. Because the lessons build on one another, they should be presented in sequential order, even if you do not use every lesson.

Reproduce the appropriate student materials. Each lesson includes both student and leader material. The student materials include information about the topic, a *What You Have Learned* section (which requires the students to write answers to questions), and *Discussion Questions.* The appropriate pages should be reproduced for each student before the start of the lesson.

Students should keep the papers used in each session in a notebook or folder for future reference.

PRESENTING THE PROGRAM

Each lesson includes a complete step-by-step *Leader's Guide,* which can be followed exactly or used as a complement to other materials.

VIOLENCE AND ITS CONSEQUENCES

|1|
What Is Violence?

|2|
Forms of Violence

|3|
Causes of Violence

|4|
Television and Violence

|5|
The Impact of Television and Movie Violence

|6|
What Is Juvenile Crime?

|7|
Being a Kid Isn't Easy

WHAT IS VIOLENCE?
(LEADER'S GUIDE)

MATERIALS NEEDED:

For each student:

- Copy of *What is Violence?* (pages 12-13)
- Pencil

LESSON:

Tell the students:

The purpose of this program is to educate students about violence, regardless of where they live. Crime is no longer restricted to the inner city. We hear stories about 5- and 6-year-old children bringing guns and other weapons to school. Child abuse is also in the news a lot. We hear about school-age children being killed by gangs and in cross-fires, and we hear of students who have gone berserk and killed children in their neighborhoods or in their schools. Crime is everywhere today.

In order to survive in a world of violence, you must know how to prevent violence from happening to you and the ones you love. You need to know how to avoid violence and how to handle violence when you cannot avoid it.

Distribute a copy of the reproduced materials (pages 12-13) and a pencil to each student. Tell the students to read *What is Violence?* and then complete the *What You Have Learned* section and answer the *Discussion Question*. Set a time limit for this activity. When the allotted time is up, have the students share their lists of different types of violence. Possible answers are:

1. domestic violence (violence in the family)
2. community violence
3. confrontational violence (violence between people who know one another)
4. gun violence
5. drug- and alcohol-related violence
6. sexual violence (rape, incest, date rape)
7. racial violence (hate crimes against members of ethnic groups or religious denominations, people whose sexual orientation is different from one's own, or those who have physical or mental disabilities).

Then have the students share their ideas about the *Discussion Question:* "Why do you think crime has reached suburban areas, small towns, and rural communities?" Be sure the discussion includes the following ideas:

- All people have dreams of and desires for a better life.

- In the hope of changing their life-styles and to escape the crime found in larger cities, people fled the inner cities and moved, with their families, to the suburbs.

- Some of the families fleeing the inner city included young people who belonged to gangs.

- Many people did not realize that other families with teens who belonged to gangs had the same hopes and ideas and also moved from the inner city. This helped spread crime to small towns, rural communities, and suburban areas. In fact, some inner-city areas are now safer than some suburbs.

Have the students put their completed papers into their notebooks to save for their own personal future reference.

WHAT IS VIOLENCE?

Violence is defined as rough or injurious physical force or power.

Violence is a word we hear a lot these days. We hear it in school. We see it demonstrated on television. We read about it in the newspaper. Although violence is not limited to the poor and working class, these people are the most dramatically affected by it.

Violence is everywhere.

At one time, inner cities were the only areas plagued by crime and violence. Today, however, suburbs of large cities, small towns, and rural areas are also affected by violence. No area is immune.

Violence is in the home.

There are many types of violence. The most familiar type of violence is the one closest to us—domestic violence. Domestic violence occurs when family members fight and try to hurt each other. When adults hurt children, it is called *child abuse.*

Child abuse is a familiar term today. We hear about child abuse happening almost every day and in every kind of family. You, or someone you know, may have been a victim of child abuse. Child abuse is wrong, and people who hurt children should be reported to authorities and punished. Sometimes parents who hurt innocent children need counseling to help them learn how to be better parents and handle the stresses that accompany being parents.

Violence occurs in the community.

Community violence includes assaults, batteries, and burglaries.

- *Robbery* is when something of value is taken from another person or from his/her immediate control by force or the threat of force.
- *Burglary* occurs when an unauthorized person enters a vehicle or structure with the intent of taking property. (In a burglary, the property is taken from the vehicle or structure. In a robbery, it is taken from the person.)
- *Assault* is a deliberate act that puts another person in fear of immediate physical harm. No physical contact is required in committing an assault.
- *Battery* is intentional, offensive physical contact committed by one person against another.

Sexual violence is a physical act of aggression or force or the threat of force which involves the touching of another's intimate parts, or forcing a person to touch another person's intimate parts. Sexual violence includes rape, incest, and date rape.

We also hear about *hate violence,* which consists of hate crimes against members of ethnic groups (racial violence) or religious denominations, people whose sexual orientation is different from one's own, or those who have physical or mental disabilities.

WHAT YOU HAVE LEARNED

There are many types of violence. List as many as you can.

1. _____
2. _____
3. _____
4. _____
5. _____
6. _____
7. _____

DISCUSSION QUESTION

Read the following question. Jot down some of your ideas. Be prepared to discuss your ideas.

Why do you think crime has reached suburban areas, small towns, and rural communities?

FORMS OF VIOLENCE
(LEADER'S GUIDE)

MATERIALS NEEDED:

For each student:

- Copy of *Forms of Violence* (pages 16-17)
- Dictionary
- Pencil

LESSON:

Tell the students:

The purpose of this lesson is to educate students about the different forms of violence. In the previous lesson, you learned that violence is wrong and that it hurts people. Being aware of various forms of violence will help you recognize when and if you have been a victim of violence.

Remember: In order to survive in a world of violence, you must be educated to prevent violence from happening to you and the ones you love. You need to know how to avoid violence and how to handle violence if you cannot avoid it.

Distribute a copy of the reproduced materials (pages 16-17), a dictionary, and a pencil to each student. Tell the students to read the *Forms of Violence*, then complete the *What You Have Learned* section and answer the *Discussion Questions*. Set a time limit for this activity. When the allotted time is up, have the students share their lists and answers. Possible answers for *What You Have Learned* are:

VIOLENT WORDS	VIOLENT ACTIONS
Name-calling	Shoving
Swearing at someone	Hitting someone
Threatening to hurt someone	Kicking someone
Shouting insults	Tripping someone
Leaving obscene messages on an answering	Robbing or stealing
machine, or calling someone and hanging up	Stabbing or shooting

1. Define *modeling*.

    Modeling is copying or imitating the action(s) of another person.

2.-5. *Accept any appropriate answers.*

Discuss the answers the students have written for the *Discussion Questions*. Include the following information for each question, if it has not been contributed by the students.

1. What do you think can be done to break the cycle of violence?

    Teach children stress-management and coping skills.

    Teach children other alternatives to punishment, like discipline. (Note: Have the students look up the meaning of discipline and punishment and explain how these concepts are alike or different.)

    Talk about your problems.

    Let children know that everyone becomes stressed out at some point.

    Learn mechanisms to handle stress, such as walking away or avoiding stressful situations or people, counting to 10 or 100, relaxing your mind, and thinking about calm and relaxing places and people.

    Have someone to talk with about your problems.

2. Why do you think some parents abuse their children?

    Parents sometimes abuse children because they don't have stress-management and coping skills. People who don't have these skills do not know appropriate ways to vent their stress or anger and often take their anger out on the people closest to them—family members and loved ones.

3. If parents who abuse their children later become ill or aged, how might they then be treated by their grown children?

    Children might treat their parents the same way they were treated by their parents.

4. Do you know of a rap group that uses lyrics that degrade women or people of specific ethnic or racial groups? If so, in what ways might that music influence you?

    Although you may not realize it, listening to music with negative undertones directly or indirectly affects your thinking. Negative messages—either from music, friends, or family members—affects the way you feel about yourself.

Have the students put their completed papers into their notebooks to save for their own personal future reference.

FORMS OF VIOLENCE

We know certain things about violence.

We've defined and discussed the different types of violence. We know that violence is wrong and that it hurts people. We also know that:

- Young people who grow up in homes where they see adults being violent are more likely than others to become violent adults and victims of violent crimes.
- Violent juveniles and adults are more likely than others to commit crimes and be sent to jail or to juvenile facilities.
- Children model themselves after their parents and other people in their immediate environment.

Modeling is a powerful learning tool.

Modeling is imitating or copying the action(s) of another. If we like the example another person is setting, we copy it. Modeling is a powerful learning tool. When parents punish by doing things like spanking with a belt, striking with an iron or extension cord, or punching with a fist, they are modeling and reinforcing negative behavior to their children. Children who are punished in this way are more likely than others to grow up to treat their children in a similar manner. In the same way, children learn how to get along with other people, how to behave, and how to value learning by modeling their parents, peers, and siblings. They can learn to act aggressively by watching violence on television and by playing violent video games.

Abused children often become abusers of their elderly parents.

The cycle does not end there. Abused children are victims when they are young and often become offenders when they are older. As their parents grow older and need to be cared for, these abused children often abuse the parents who abused them. Parents need to realize that if they become a part of this vicious cycle, they may some day be at the mercy of their children. Everyone needs to be more aware of the relationship between abuse and delinquency. The scars and pain of abuse don't go away without the intervention of counseling by trained professionals.

Abused boys often develop abusive relationships with girls and women.

Boys who witness abuse or who are themselves abused, are often abusive in their relationships with girls and women. This abuse can be verbal or physical. References to abuse can be found in many rap songs and movies which degrade and exploit women or members of various racial or ethnic groups.

WHAT YOU HAVE LEARNED

List as many examples of violent words and violent actions as you can.

VIOLENT WORDS	VIOLENT ACTIONS
1. _____	1. _____
2. _____	2. _____
3. _____	3. _____
4. _____	4. _____
5. _____	5. _____
6. _____	6. _____
7. _____	7. _____
8. _____	8. _____
9. _____	9. _____
10. _____	10. _____

Answer the statements below, based on what you have learned about modeling.

1. Define *modeling*.

2. Give one example of how your teacher models for you.

3. Give one example of how your parent models for you.

4. Give one example of how another close relative whom you like models for you.

5. If you have a younger brother or sister, give an example of how you model for him/her.

DISCUSSION QUESTIONS

1. What do you think can be done to break the cycle of violence?

2. Why do you think some parents abuse their children?

3. If parents who abuse their children later become ill or aged, how might they then be treated by their grown children?

4. Do you know of a rap group that uses lyrics that degrade women or people of specific ethnic or racial groups? If you do, in what ways might that music influence you?

131
CAUSES OF VIOLENCE
(LEADER'S GUIDE)

MATERIALS NEEDED:

For each student:

I   Copy of *Causes of Violence* (pages 20-21)
I   Pencil

LESSON:

Tell the students:

> The purpose of this lesson is to examine some of the reasons why violence occurs. One cause of violence is *stalking*. Another is the *loss of self-control*. Many different feelings can cause a person to lose self-control. By becoming aware of these feelings and linking them with certain experiences you have had, you will better understand the reasons why you may lose self-control. By understanding these "triggers," you may learn to exercise more self-control.

Distribute a copy of the reproduced materials (pages 20-21) and a pencil to each student. Tell the students to read *Causes of Violence* and use the definitions to write the sentences in the *What You Have Learned* section. Then have them write their opinions for the *Discussion Questions*. Set a time limit for this activity. When the allotted time is up, have the students share their answers to the questions. Their answers should relate to the following definitions:

1. *Anger* occurs when something or someone seems unfair. We become scared when we feel threatened or in danger. Everyone has experienced being angry and feeling fear.

2. *Disappointment* occurs when someone breaks a promise or fails us in some other way. With busy schedules, parents sometimes make promises they later find that they can't keep. When this happens, we feel disappointed. When we experience too many disappointments, we can lose hope and lose self-control.

3. *Sadness* occurs when we lose something or someone close to us. When a pet dies or a friend moves away, we feel sad.

4. *Embarrassment* or *hurt* occurs when someone around us makes fun of us or ridicules us. When this happens, it is hard to remember that people who make fun of others generally have been hurt and don't feel good about themselves.

5. *Excitement* is what we feel when we become agitated or stirred up emotionally.

6. *Boredom* is what we feel when we become uninterested in or tired of something. Boredom is one reason why young people join gangs and end up hanging around with the wrong crowd. Boredom is less likely to occur if neighborhoods have youth centers and activities to keep young people involved in constructive, worthwhile activities.

7. *Frustration* occurs when we are disappointed. This may be from having plans changed by another person or from repeatedly trying to do something without success.

8. *Depression* occurs when we are in a bad situation and can see no way out.

Have the students share their ideas about the *Discussion Questions*.

1. Have you ever experienced racism?

    Accept any appropriate answers.

2. How does your family feel about members of other racial, ethnic, or religious groups?

    Accept any appropriate answers.

3. If families are prejudiced against members of other racial, ethnic, or religious groups, how might this feeling consciously or unconsciously influence a person's thinking and beliefs?

    Accept any appropriate answers.

Have the students put their completed papers into their notebooks to save for their own personal future reference.

OPTIONAL ACTIVITY:

Write each of the 10 feelings from *What You Have Learned* on a 3" x 5" card. Select 10 students and pass each of them a card. Tell the students not to reveal what is written on their cards. Select a short poem or nursery rhyme. Tell the students with the cards that each of them is to recite the selected piece as if he/she were experiencing the feeling written on his/her card. Tell the other students that they are to guess what feeling is being portrayed.

When each of the 10 students has finished reciting, tell the students:

By recognizing feelings that occur within yourself or others, you will be better able to recognize when a feeling that can lead to the loss of self-control is taking place. This knowledge will help you control yourself and avoid others who may be in danger of losing self-control.

CAUSES OF VIOLENCE

Violence is found everywhere.

Some people in our society attribute violence to unemployment, illiteracy, poverty, drugs, child abuse, and gangs. But not all violent people live in poor neighborhoods. There is violence among the rich and middle class as well as the poor. There is violence in the suburbs and in rural areas as well as in the inner city. Violence knows no boundaries. Children killing children, children killing adults, adults killing children, youth-on-youth crimes, and adults killing adults are types of violent crimes reported in the news and portrayed on television.

Stalking often leads to violence.

Stalking is defined as the tracking/pursuit of game animals or other victims. The purpose of stalking is to pursue or approach prey in a threatening way in order to frighten or cause harm. So many cases of stalking have been reported that it became necessary to pass a law that makes it illegal for one person to stalk another.

Violence comes about when a person loses self-control.

Self-control means being in charge of yourself and having the ability to control your feelings, thoughts, and actions. Negative feelings can cause a person to lose self-control. Some of the negative feelings that can cause the loss of self-control are fear, anger, disappointment, sadness, embarrassment, excitement, boredom, frustration, and depression.

Everyone has had or will experience these feelings in life, but that doesn't mean that everyone is going to become violent. Many people know how to cope with negative feelings and control their behavior when these feelings occur. Others become stressed out when these feelings occur. When this happens, the combination of stress and exaggerated feelings such as anger, frustration, or depression causes them to lose control of their actions and contributes to a state of violence.

Losing self-control occurs when emotions take over the ability to think clearly and reason.

Take some time to think about each of the feelings that can cause loss of self-control.

Anger occurs when something or someone seems unfair. We become scared when we feel threatened or in danger. Everyone has experienced being angry and feeling fear.

Disappointment occurs when someone breaks a promise or fails us in some other way. With busy schedules, parents sometimes make promises they later find that they can't keep. When this happens, we feel disappointed. When we experience too many disappointments, we can lose hope and lose self-control.

Sadness occurs when we lose something or someone close to us. When a pet dies or a friend moves away, we feel sad.

Embarrassment or *hurt* occurs when someone around us makes fun of us or ridicules us. When this happens, it is hard to remember that people who make fun of others generally have been hurt and don't feel good about themselves.

Excitement is what we feel when we become agitated or stirred up emotionally.

Boredom is what we feel when we become uninterested in or tired of something. Boredom is one reason why young people join gangs and end up hanging around with the wrong crowd. Boredom is less likely to occur if neighborhoods have youth centers and activities to keep young people involved in constructive, worthwhile activities.

Frustration occurs when we are disappointed. This may be from having plans changed by another person or from repeatedly trying to do something without success.

Depression occurs when we are in a bad situation and can see no way out.

WHAT YOU HAVE LEARNED

To better understand each of the feelings you have just read about, write a sentence about each of the words below.

1. Fear
2. Anger
3. Disappointment
4. Sadness
5. Hurt
6. Embarrassment
7. Excitement
8. Boredom
9. Frustration
10. Depression

Write about a time when you were upset but kept your self-control.

DISCUSSION QUESTIONS

1. Have you ever experienced racism?

2. How does your family feel about members of other racial, ethnic, or religious groups?

3. If families are prejudiced against members of other racial, ethnic, or religious groups, how might this feeling consciously or unconsciously influence a person's thinking and beliefs?

141
TELEVISION AND VIOLENCE
(LEADER'S GUIDE)

MATERIALS NEEDED:

For each student:

- Copy of *Television and Violence* (page 23)
- Pencil

For the leader:

- VCR
- 15-minute taped segment of a televised cartoon

LESSON:

Tell the students:

The purpose of this lesson is to help you become aware of the amount of violence broadcast on television.

Distribute a copy of the reproduced material (page 23) and a pencil to each student. Ask the students to complete the questionnaire. Set a time limit for this activity. When the allotted time is up, tally the answers. Then ask the students to discuss whether they make most of the choices or their parents control what they watch. Determine the reasons for the students' answers.

Tell the students that you are going to show a 15-minute segment from a cartoon shown on television. Ask them to make a check or a stroke each time a violent scene occurs. Show the tape, then ask the students for their results. Then have the students answer the following questions:

1. What does this tell you about watching cartoons?

2. How do you think the amount of violence in cartoons compares with the amount of violence in other shows?

Have the students put their completed papers into their notebooks to save for their own personal future reference.

TELEVISION AND VIOLENCE

WHAT YOU HAVE LEARNED

Complete the survey below. After everyone has finished, the scores will be tallied and you will see the results of your class vote. Circle as many answers as are appropriate for you.

1. Who picks the programs you watch on TV?   YOU   MOM   DAD   OTHER

2. Who picks the videos rented in your home?   YOU   MOM   DAD   OTHER

3. Who usually controls the remote control in your home?   YOU   MOM   DAD   OTHER

4. Do you have cable in your home?   YES   NO

    If you have cable, who selected the channels?   YOU   MOM   DAD   OTHER

5. Do you have channels blocked on your cable?   YES   NO

    Who blocked them?   YOU   MOM   DAD   OTHER

6. When you are being punished, are you allowed to watch TV?   YES   NO

    If you are not allowed to watch TV,

    who monitors to make sure you don't watch?   YOU   MOM   DAD   OTHER

THE IMPACT OF TELEVISION AND MOVIE VIOLENCE
(LEADER'S GUIDE)

MATERIALS NEEDED:

For each student:

- Copy of *The Impact of Television and Movie Violence* (pages 25-27)
- Pencil

For the leader:

- Several copies of movie guides from local newspapers

LESSON:

Tell the students:

> The purpose of this lesson is to help you understand that one cause of violence is linked to viewing violent television programs and violent movies. These programs are thought to motivate young people to imitate the aggression seen on the screen. Young people who frequently watch violent television programs and movies can begin to believe that violence is normal and acceptable behavior. Young people who watch violent television programs and movies accept obscene language as the norm and use it themselves. In homes where parents do not watch a lot of violent programs, the percentage of young people who see violent television programs and videos decreases dramatically.

Distribute a copy of the reproduced materials (pages 25-27) and a pencil to each student. Tell the students to read *The Impact of Television and Movie Violence* and complete the *What You Have Learned* section. Have movie guides available for the students to use when they are ready to do that section of the activity. If there are not enough movie guides for each student to have one, allow the students to share the guides while doing this portion of the assignment. Set a time limit for this activity. When the allotted time is up, ask the students to share their answers with the group.

Possible answers for the first section on rating symbols are:

1. G — *General Audiences*
2. R — *Under 16, not admitted without a parent or guardian*
3. NC-17 — *No children under 17 allowed, which replaced the X rating*
4. PG-13 — *Parental guidance suggested for children under 13*

Have the students put their completed papers into their notebooks to save for their own personal future reference.

THE IMPACT OF TELEVISION AND MOVIE VIOLENCE

Violence on television and in movies is linked to violent behaviors.

One cause of violence is linked to viewing violent television and movies. Young people are impressionable, and aggressive behavior on television and movies may trigger them to imitate what they see. You were not born violent, but when you are exposed to an excessive amount of television and movie violence, you can become desensitized to violence. This means that aggressive actions like pushing, shoving, knocking over others' toys, scratching, kicking, pulling hair, and taking others' possessions are seen as normal and acceptable behaviors.

When you watch violent television and movies, you are likely to accept obscene language as the norm and imitate it. Exposure to violence on television and in movies can also validate prejudiced attitudes about the roles of men and women, minority groups, the poor, and young people. If you are a member of a minority group, seeing minority groups portrayed in a negative way can influence the way you think about yourself.

Because viewing violence has so many implications, you are wise to learn all you can about what could happen if you became absorbed in violent media. Ignore the temptation to say, "It might happen to other kids, but not to me." That sentence has been uttered too many times by too many young people who ended up in trouble or dead.

Parents set the tone for their children's television and movie viewing.

Parents' attitudes toward their children's viewing habits and video games have a major influence over what children see and do. Parents who set limits on the amount of time children view television are helping their children establish good viewing patterns. In homes where parents themselves watch violent television programs or videos, they expose their children to the same violence. These children learn that it's okay to view violent programs, and they run the risk of becoming desensitized to the importance of human life. In homes where parents do not watch high numbers of violent programs, the percentage of children who see violent television programs and videos decreases dramatically.

Television and movies may affect self-esteem.

Forty years ago, when people listened to radio programs and heard only voices, self-esteem was not as much an issue as it is today. Radio listeners did not see the faces or bodies of the people whose voices they heard. There were no visual images for the listeners to compare themselves with or measure themselves against.

Television and movies may indirectly affect your self-esteem by causing you to compare yourself with the beautiful faces and bodies you see on the screen. You need to wise up and realize that these people are actors and actresses and that, off-screen, they have some of the same concerns and problems as everyone else.

Violent television programs and movies leave lasting impressions.

Violent television programs and movies leave indelible impressions on young people and can have a very destructive impact on them. They are not viewed and forgotten. Young children exposed to violent television and videos have more nightmares, are more afraid of the dark, and are more fearful of being left alone. These children are often more insecure and report feelings of being "scared." They are also more apt to be nervous and to have personal insecurities that affect their relationships with peers and their school performance.

Most television does not require interaction.

Language development is one of the most important skills you need to acquire. You need to be able to interact in a positive way with people in order to get along with your peers, hold down a job, and, in the future, be a good parent. Studies have shown that children acquire very little language development from viewing television. This is probably because most television does not require interaction. You do not have to involve yourself in television. You just have to *be there*. There is no interaction or exchange of ideas.

You are living in the television-video-computer generation. These media compete with homework, family activities, and non-media-type games. Many times, television or video games are played to avoid boredom. If you watch TV because you are bored, then you need to look at what is happening in your life and decide how you can change it. There are many alternatives to boredom other than television and videos. Look around your community and neighborhood to find ways that you can become involved with people in activities that will help you improve your self-esteem. Volunteerism, socializing with friends, and joining a club or participating in a sport can eliminate boredom and help you find nonviolent ways of interacting with those around you.

When used correctly, television and movies can be wonderful tools of communication.

The media can be a great learning tool. If you use it correctly, it can help you learn many things about the world around you. Be smart. Don't get caught in the media game that glorifies violent language and behavior. See through the propaganda and refuse to be sucked into it. Choose your video games, television programs, and movies for their entertainment value, not for their violence.

WHAT YOU HAVE LEARNED

Some of the symbols listed below are ones that you already know. Write their meanings on the lines provided.

1. G _____
2. R _____
3. NC-17 _____
4. PG-13 _____

Look at a movie guide from a local newspaper. See what movies use the ratings above. In the space below, write the name of a movie, then write the rating next to it.

List as many alternatives to watching television or playing video games as you can think of. Your goal is to name 10 alternatives. Can you do it?

1. _____
2. _____
3. _____
4. _____
5. _____
6. _____
7. _____
8. _____
9. _____
10. _____

WHAT IS JUVENILE CRIME?
(LEADER'S GUIDE)

MATERIALS NEEDED:

For each student:

- Copy of *What is Juvenile Crime?* (pages 30-31)
- Dictionary
- Pencil

LESSON:

Tell the students:

The purpose of this lesson is to define and learn the differences between *juvenile crime* and *adult crime* and *juvenile court* and *adult court*. You will also identify some positive and some negative characteristics about yourself and discuss what gets students into trouble both at home and in school.

Distribute a copy of the reproduced materials (pages 30-31), a dictionary, and a pencil to each student. Tell the students to read *What is Juvenile Crime?* and then complete the *What You Have Learned* and *Discussion Question* sections. Set a time limit for this activity.

When the allotted time is up, have the students share their answers to the questions. There are no right or wrong answers to any of the questions, and you should accept any reasonable answer submitted by a student.

Then have the students give their definitions. The definitions are as follows:

1. Crime

    Any serious violation of a society's laws

2. Juvenile crime

    A serious wrongdoing committed by a young person

3. Juvenile delinquency

    Any illegal or antisocial behavior on the part of a minor

4. Juvenile court

   A court of law having jurisdiction over minors (Minors *generally refers to those under 18 years of age.*)

Discuss the students' opinions about the *Discussion Question*.

Have the students put their completed papers into their notebooks to save for their own personal future reference.

WHAT IS JUVENILE CRIME?

Do you believe *crime* and *violence* are the same?

Crime is defined as any serious violation of a society's laws. A *crime* is a serious wrongdoing. Whenever a crime takes place, the law has the right to punish the person who committed the crime. When gangs, drugs, and abuse are present, they are generally linked with crime.

What is a *juvenile crime*?

We hear a lot about *juvenile crime* on the news and in newspapers.

A *juvenile* is defined simply as a young person. A *juvenile crime* is a crime committed by a young person.

What is *juvenile delinquency*?

Juvenile delinquency is any illegal or antisocial behavior on the part of a minor. Juvenile delinquency is handled in juvenile court. Forms of juvenile delinquency include: robbery, aggravated assault, motor-vehicle theft, murder, arson, vandalism, defying liquor laws, and drug abuse.

What is a *juvenile court*?

Juvenile court is a court of law having jurisdiction over minors (generally those under 18 years of age).

Laws for juveniles differ from state to state. Youth-on-youth crime—young people committing criminal acts against people their own age—is on the rise. Young people are also preying on the elderly. Because so many crimes are being committed by young people today, many states are attempting to pass laws to try children as young as 11 or 12 as adults when they commit violent crimes—generally those that involve ending human life. When juveniles are tried as adults, their cases are tried in criminal court, just like those of adults, and carry the same type of penalty as crimes committed by adults.

WHAT YOU HAVE LEARNED

List four things you think are good about yourself.

1. _____
2. _____
3. _____
4. _____

List four things you'd like to improve about yourself.

1. _____
2. _____
3. _____
4. _____

Answer the following questions. Your answers to these questions will help you better understand yourself.

1. What gets you into trouble in school?

2. What gets you into trouble at home?

Explain in your own words what the following terms mean. You may use a dictionary.

1. Crime

2. Juvenile crime

3. Juvenile delinquency

4. Juvenile court

DISCUSSION QUESTION

Do you believe *crime* and *violence* are the same? Explain your answer.

7
BEING A KID ISN'T EASY
(LEADER'S GUIDE)

MATERIALS NEEDED:

For each student:

- Copy of *Being a Kid Isn't Easy* (page 34)

For each student group:

- Copy of *Discussion Questions* (page 35)
- Pencil
- Newspaper articles (brought in by the students or the leader) relating to a violent crime committed by a person the students' own age

LESSON:

Tell the students:

> The purpose of this lesson is to discuss how children growing up in today's world face more challenging times than their parents and grandparents did. We all have read and seen some shocking but real accounts of the ugliness that faces kids today. It is not uncommon for third- and fourth-grade students in large cities to have personally witnessed some form of violence. Even though recent statistics from the Office of Juvenile Justice and Delinquency Prevention report that the percentage of juvenile crimes has decreased, the figures are still startling. Between 1988 and 1997, the overall juvenile arrest rate increased 22%. A lot of young people today feel that their lives aren't worth much.

Distribute a copy of *Being a Kid Isn't Easy* (page 34) to each student. Ask the students to read the information on the page. Set a time limit for this activity.

Divide the students into small groups. Give each group a copy of the *Discussion Questions* (page 35). Select a leader and a recorder for each group. Explain that the leader's responsibility is to make sure that the discussion is conducted in an orderly manner and that the recorder's responsibility is to take notes on the opinions of the group members. The recorder should be prepared to share his/her group's opinions with the rest of the class. Have each group discuss the first three *Discussion Questions*. Set a time limit for this and have the recorders report back to the entire class when the allotted time is up. Then distribute newspaper or magazine articles to each of the groups. Have each group discuss the final *Discussion Question*. Set a time limit for this and have the recorders report back to the entire class when the allotted time is up.

Have the students put their completed papers into their notebooks to save for their own personal future reference.

OPTIONAL ASSIGNMENT:

Tell the students:

> Select a city like Chicago or New York or your own community and write two or three paragraphs about its juvenile laws. Tell whether you feel the laws are outdated and need to be changed or are acceptable as they are. Be prepared to share your article and your opinion with the rest of the class.

Set a due date.

BEING A KID ISN'T EASY

Kids today face shocking, real-life violence.

In one year, students entered a middle school, more than one high school, and a school function and shot and killed fellow students and teachers. Arrest rates for juvenile offenders under the age of 17 have greatly increased for homicide, aggravated assault, and juvenile rape.

These are shocking but real accounts of the ugliness facing today's kids. We know that most children don't shoot other children, but one such crime is one too many.

Children who personally witness random acts of violence face the possibility of being emotionally scarred.

Large numbers of third- and fourth-grade students in large cities have personally witnessed some form of violence. They have seen home invasions, domestic violence, stabbings, shootings, gang attacks, car accidents and car break-ins, and drive-by shootings. Many are subjected to a daily dose of verbal violence and abuse. Children who personally witness such violent acts face the possibility of being emotionally scarred. A lot of young people today feel that their lives aren't worth much. They see people their age dying violent deaths and wonder if they will ever reach the age of 18.

Most state juvenile codes are long overdue for change.

Today's juvenile criminals are more dangerous than the juvenile delinquents who, 35 years ago, stole a car and took it for a joy ride or stole a car's hubcaps. The juvenile laws in effect today do not work, because they were designed for another time. Today, some 10- and 11-year-olds are committing murders and receiving five years' probation in the custody of their parents. Do you think the family of the person who was murdered believes this is fair punishment for the crime? If someone you knew was murdered, would you think this was fair punishment for the crime?

DISCUSSION QUESTIONS

1. What should be done to punish young people 9, 10, 11 years old and older who take someone's life?

2. Should the courts give someone like this a light sentence or should he/she be tried as an adult? Before you come to a conclusion, think about the victims and the victims' families.

3. Think about the young person who committed the crime and his/her family. What can be done to prevent this kind of tragedy from happening in the future?

4. Share your thoughts with your group about the newspaper or magazine article involving a person about the same age as you who was involved in a crime.

THE IMPORTANCE OF FAMILY VALUES

| 8 |
Families

| 9 |
Family Rules

| 10 |
You and Your Family

FAMILIES
(LEADER'S GUIDE)

MATERIALS NEEDED:

For each student:

- Copy of *Families* (pages 40-41)
- Pencil

Note: This lesson can be expanded by using newspaper clippings or articles on family values, gender crimes, information to support male-female violence, or the increase in female participation in violent crimes. These articles may be brought in by the students or supplied by the leader.

LESSON:

Tell the students:

The purpose of this lesson is to help you understand the role that family, friends, and the community play in shaping your self-image and the importance of family values in our society. Most often, parents who set limits and have family rules produce children who have high self-esteem. We are also going to discuss the importance of male role-models for boys, the ways in which boys have traditionally been raised, and the importance of family values.

Show the students the newspaper clippings and have them describe how these pictures may relate to a family-value system. (Optional)

Distribute a copy of the reproduced materials (pages 40-41) and a pencil to each student. Tell the students to read *Families,* then write answers to the questions under the *What You Have Learned* section. Set a time limit for this activity. When the allotted time is up, have the students share their answers to the questions. Possible answers are:

1. Why have boys traditionally been more aggressive than girls?

    Boys have traditionally been raised to be more aggressive than girls, but this is changing. Male role-models (movie actors, sports stars) have also modeled more aggressive behavior than traditional female role-models.

2. What can be done to change this stereotyping in our society?

    Accept any reasonable answer. Possible answers could include: Teach boys that it is OK to cry and express emotions, to enjoy sports for sports' sake without being competitive, that toughness and manhood are not the same.

3. What is necessary in our society to curb or end violence?

    Family values are necessary in society to curb violence.

4. How do children raised in a community surrounded by violence, guns, and crime have a good chance of turning out?

    They will have little chance of not committing violent acts and becoming criminals.

5. Why do children who are hugged and told they are loved probably turn out differently than children who don't receive these assurances?

    A child who knows he/she is loved will most likely develop a good self-image which will help him/her avoid criminal and violent acts.

6. Should the rules for boys and girls be the same in a household, or should rules for boys differ from those for girls?

    Accept any reasonable answers.

7. What is meant by: "It takes a community to raise a child"?

    It means everyone has a responsibility for everyone else. (The original wording—It takes a village to raise a child—is an African tribal saying.)

Have the students put their completed papers into their notebooks to save for their own personal future reference.

FAMILIES

Families play an important part in the way children see themselves and whether they develop violent behavior.

The way children believe other people see them—especially their families and friends—helps to shape their self-image and self-esteem. Families who are supportive and love their children unconditionally are most likely to have children with high self-esteem. Families who constantly put their children down are more likely to have children with low self-esteem. This is because children who constantly hear uncomplimentary things about themselves soon begin to believe they are worthless. Children who believe they are worthless are more likely to express their negative feelings in violent behavior.

Children with high self-esteem are more likely to have parents who set limits and have rules that are respected and followed in the home. These parents don't allow their children to be disrespectful and talk back to them or to other adults. Children with low self-esteem are more likely to come from families where there are few rules and few or no limits. In these families the parents are more permissive, letting their children get away with things like breaking curfews.

Does this mean that your family is responsible for your self-esteem? NO! It only means that your family may influence your opinion of yourself.

There are many single-parent families in our society. Depending upon the roles played by the parents, these families can have special concerns. If the custodial parent is overwhelmed by emotional and/or financial circumstances or has a limited knowledge of setting rules and limits, the household is likely to be permissive. If not, a single-parent household can be as self-esteem-building as any other.

Boys need male role-models. If the father—who should be the role-model for his sons—is absent from the family, a new set of problems may arise. It is a known fact that the absence of fathers in child-rearing is linked to male violence. Boys raised by both parents to be nurturing, caring fathers are less likely to turn to violence. However, boys surrounded by women in homes, in schools, and in the community may become saturated by and resentful of female authority figures.

Does this mean that a male whose father is absent from the home has the right to be violent? NO! It only means that he will need to find another male role-model to take his father's place. We are all personally responsible for the choices we make.

Divorce sometimes makes adults bitter and revengeful. This is not the child's fault, but the child may feel the effects of the bitterness. For example, a custodial parent who shares the financial and emotional child-rearing responsibility with a supportive ex-spouse may be more loving and caring than a custodial parent on his/her own who is often resentful and angry at the child's non-supportive absent parent.

Does this mean that the custodial parent with a supportive ex-spouse loves his/her children more than the one with a non-supportive ex-spouse? NO! It means that the custodial parent who does not have a supportive ex-spouse is so busy trying to keep everyone's life together that he/she doesn't have the energy to be as attentive as the one who has a supportive ex-spouse.

In our society, it is easy to raise children to be aggressive and violent. At the present time, there tends to be more violence among boys than among girls. However, this trend may change as the number of girls involved in violent acts increases. Why is this so? Traditionally, boys have been raised to be more aggressive and were rewarded for aggressive behavior more often than girls were. This reward for male aggression can be seen in how boys are raised to be tougher and less sensitive than girls. It is seen in how boys are taught to win in sports, at whatever cost, and to develop a connection between manhood and toughness. This need for toughness and destructive aggression is evidenced by boys' desire for war games and guns, violent video games, and playing with toy monster/action figures. What is the message boys learn? They learn that it is OK to hurt others.

Does this mean that girls are not aggressive in sports, don't like violent video games, and do not play with toy monster/action figures? NO! It means that, traditionally, these things have been done primarily by boys.

Families can discourage violent behavior.

First, it is necessary to recognize the importance of family values. Each family has its own set of values, which may be the same as or different from another family's. All families do not have to think alike, but a value system is necessary for our culture's survival.

Second, we need communities and neighborhoods to act as extended families. When your parent is busy in the house or away from home and your next-door neighbor sees you doing wrong, he/she should feel free to tell you to stop what you are doing. As it now stands, many neighbors say nothing because they fear retaliation from the parent, the child, or both. Neighbors used to watch out for one another, and families in communities used to work together. When families work together, they make neighborhoods strong. Strong neighborhoods make strong communities. Strong communities will make a strong country. It takes a community to raise a child.

WHAT YOU HAVE LEARNED

1. Why have boys traditionally been more aggressive than girls?

2. What can be done to change this stereotyping in our society?

3. What is necessary in our society to curb or end violence?

4. How do children raised in a community surrounded by violence, guns, and crime have a good chance of turning out?

5. Why do children who are hugged and told they are loved probably turn out differently than children who don't receive these assurances?

6. Should the rules for boys and girls be the same in a household, or should rules for boys differ from those for girls?

7. What is meant by: "It takes a community to raise a child"?

FAMILY RULES
(LEADER'S GUIDE)

MATERIALS NEEDED:

For each student:

- Copy of *Family Rules* (page 43)
- Pencil
- Art paper and crayons or markers (optional)

LESSON:

Tell the students:

> The purpose of this lesson is to help you understand that boundaries and limit-setting (rules) are necessary structures in any environment. There are rules to obey at home, at school, and in public buildings. There are even rules to obey at church and while visiting other people's homes. There are driving rules and rules in the workplace. Rules are designed to keep everyone safe and to maintain order.

Distribute a copy of the reproduced material (page 43) and a pencil to each student. Tell the students to complete the questionnaire. Set a time limit for this activity. When the allotted time is up, have the students share their answers. (If desired and appropriate, tell the students that five or more "No" answers indicate that there is not enough supervision in their lives and that some adult needs to be responsible for providing more structure and limit-setting.) Tell the students:

> If you would like any of the "No" answers to be "Yes," discuss the situation with your parents.

Have the students put their completed papers into their notebooks to save for their own personal future reference.

OPTIONAL ACTIVITY:

Prior to distributing *Family Rules*, ask the students to name different places and situations in which there are rules. Write their answers on the chalkboard. Some suggestions could be: signals for traffic, weapons regulations, and water-usage restrictions in a drought situation. Distribute art paper, pencils, and crayons or markers to each student. Tell the students to select one of the situations or places written on the chalkboard and draw a picture of what it would be like if rules about how to behave in these situations did not exist. Set a time limit for this. After everyone has finished, have the students share their drawings.

FAMILY RULES

WHAT YOU HAVE LEARNED

Directions: Read each sentence. Then put a check in the "Yes" or "No" column. When you have finished, tally the "No" answers.

		Yes	No
1.	Do you have a curfew or time to come into the house at night?	☐	☐
2.	Do you have a set time to be in bed each night?	☐	☐
3.	Are there rules about taking a bath or shower?	☐	☐
4.	Are there rules about or punishment for cursing in your home?	☐	☐
5.	Do you have assigned chores?	☐	☐
6.	Are there rules about putting dinner dishes away?	☐	☐
7.	Are there rules about when and where you do your homework?	☐	☐
8.	Is there someone who checks your homework after it is completed?	☐	☐
9.	Are there rules about being on time for school?	☐	☐
10.	Are there rules about respecting adults?	☐	☐
11.	Are there rules about fighting with brothers and sisters within the family?	☐	☐

Total "No" answers:_____

YOU AND YOUR FAMILY
(LEADER'S GUIDE)

MATERIALS NEEDED:

For each student:

- Copy of *You and Your Family* (page 45)
- Colored pencils, crayons, and/or washable markers

LESSON:

Tell the students:

> Every member of the family sees the other members differently. If you had your brother, sister, mother, or father complete the activity you are going to complete in a few moments, each picture would probably be different. We will talk about this later.

Distribute a copy of the reproduced material (page 45) and colored pencils, crayons, and/or washable markers to each student. Tell the students to follow the directions under the *What You Have Learned* section. Set a time limit for this activity. When the allotted time is up, have the students share their drawings. After the drawings have been presented, ask the students the following questions. Tell the students that the answer to some questions may be "myself."

1. Who do you see as being the strongest person in your family? Why?
2. Who do you see as being the weakest person in your family? Why?
3. Which person in your family is most like you? In what way?
4. Which person in your family is most different from you? In what way?
5. If you had a problem, which person in your family would you go to for help or advice? Why?
6. If you had a problem, which person in your family would you *not* go to for help or advice? Why?
7. Do you think every other member of your family would draw the same picture you did and answer the questions the same way? Why or why not?

Have the students put their completed papers into their notebooks to save for their own personal future reference.

YOU AND YOUR FAMILY

WHAT YOU HAVE LEARNED

Draw a picture of the members of your family. You may use colored pencils, crayons, or washable markers. Label each family member you draw. After you have finished, be prepared to discuss each family member. Remember to include yourself in the family!

Answer the following questions:

1. Who do you see as being the strongest person in your family? Why?

2. Who do you see as being the weakest person in your family? Why?

3. Which person in your family is most like you? In what way?

4. Which person in your family is most different from you? In what way?

5. If you had a problem, which person in your family would you go to for help or advice? Why?

6. If you had a problem, which person in your family would you *not* go to for help or advice? Why?

7. Do you think every other member of your family would draw the same picture you did and answer the questions the same way? Why or why not?

ANGER AND WHAT TO DO ABOUT IT

| 11 |
When Anger Takes Over—
Who's in Control?

| 12 |
Managing Anger

| 13 |
Negative Behaviors
I Need to Work on

| 14 |
Alternatives to Fighting

| 15 |
Anger Alternatives

11
WHEN ANGER TAKES OVER—WHO'S IN CONTROL?
(LEADER'S GUIDE)

MATERIALS NEEDED:

For each student:

- Copy of *When Anger Takes Over—Who's in Control?* (page 49)
- Pencil

LESSON:

Tell the students:

> The purpose of this lesson is to help you understand that when you're angry, you sometimes say and do things you later regret. This is because you lose control. When you lose control, your ability to think clearly and solve problems decreases. Think about a car and about how a car is controlled. It is controlled by a driver who turns the wheel, steps on or off the gas, and uses the brakes. What would the car be like if the driver just sat in the car and let it go its own way? The driver could end up in a ditch, the driver could be going nowhere, or the driver could be killed. Anger operates the same way. When anger takes over, you can end up getting into trouble, make no progress at all, or do something disastrous. If you want to be in control of your life, you must learn not to let anger take over when something upsets you.

Distribute a copy of the reproduced material (page 49) and a pencil to each student. Tell the students to read *When Anger Takes Over—Who's in Control?* and then complete the *What You Have Learned* section. Set a time limit for this activity. When the allotted time is up, have the students share their answers.

Ask all of the students who enjoy having someone or something control their lives and make decisions for them to stand up. Ask the students who are still sitting if they know what to do when anger controls their lives. Allow time for answers. Then tell the students that during the next lessons, they will learn more about managing anger and what they can do about their personal situations.

Have the students put their completed papers into their notebooks to save for their own personal future reference.

WHEN ANGER TAKES OVER— WHO'S IN CONTROL?

Anger causes you to lose your ability to think clearly.

When you're angry, you sometimes say and do things you later regret. This is because when anger takes over, your ability to think clearly and solve problems decreases. You feel that people are against you, and you develop negative feelings about yourself. When you feel people are against you, you will react in one of two ways—taking revenge or becoming less confident in your ability and, eventually, giving up. Either way, your self-esteem suffers. You start saying, "They have no right to do this to me. Wait until something *they* want comes along." "Why try? What's the point? I'm going to fail anyway." or "I can't do it, and anyway, nobody cares." When you take revenge on others, you don't feel good about yourself. No one else feels good about you, either. When you lose confidence in yourself, everyone else loses confidence in you, too. When this happens, who's in control? Certainly not you!

WHAT YOU HAVE LEARNED

Answer the following questions:

1. When a driver loses control of a car, who is in control: the driver or the car?
   Who *should* be in control of the car?

2. When a girl gives her lunch money to a bully, who is in control: the bully or the girl?
   Who *should* be in control of the girl's lunch money?

3. When a parent gives in to a toddler throwing a temper tantrum, who is in control: the parent or the toddler?
   Who *should* be in control?

4. When you lose your temper, break your mom's vase, and get grounded for a week, who is in control: you or your temper?
   Who *should* be in control?

5. When you get angry about a bad test grade and refuse to put in extra time studying, who is in control: you or your anger?
   Who *should* be in control?

Make a list of situations that cause you to lose control.

12
MANAGING ANGER
(LEADER'S GUIDE)

MATERIALS NEEDED:

For each student:

- Copy of *Managing Anger* (pages 52-55)
- Pencil

LESSON:

Tell the students:

> The purpose of this lesson is to help you understand that everyone experiences anger at some point. Anger is a legitimate emotion. It is the *reaction* to anger that sometimes gets people into trouble. Reactions to anger are mostly learned from people who are close to us or from people we admire. Many times, these role-models do not have good anger-management skills. If this is true for you, and you choose to, you can learn different anger-management techniques that are appropriate for healthy living.

Distribute a copy of the reproduced materials (pages 52-55) and a pencil to each student. Tell the students to read *Managing Anger* and then complete the *What You Have Learned* section. Set a time limit for this activity. When the allotted time is up, have the students share their answers. Possible answers are:

1. When people are angry, they might:

    scream, curse, hurt someone physically or verbally, lie, cheat, steal, cry, throw temper tantrums, act helpless, act as if they don't care, say things they don't mean, overeat, drink, abuse drugs, become defiant, etc.

2. Make a list of appropriate ways of expressing your anger. Use words or actions that will not hurt or belittle another person.

    1. *Attack the problem, not the person. Don't curse, call names, or hurt anyone in any way.*

    2. *Make every effort not to blame anyone, but be specific in identifying the problem.*

    3. *Listen to what the other person is saying. Don't interrupt while he/she is talking. When it is your turn, he/she should show you the same respect.*

4. *Maintain good eye contact. People trust people who look directly at them.*

5. *Use good body language. Do not stand with your arms folded, keep them at your sides. Don't frown or purse your lips. Don't stand with your head tilted to one side or your body leaning to one side.*

6. *Try to see the problem from the other person's point of view. This is hard to do, but it is important.*

7. *Ask questions. If you don't understand something, don't assume you know what the other person means. Remember: That person is standing in front of you, and this is a perfect opportunity to clear things up.*

8. *Try not to raise your voice or yell. Yelling or shouting makes you angrier and puts the other person on the defensive.*

9. *Use humor, if it's appropriate. Apologize, even if the mistake was not yours. Sometimes these techniques can diffuse an uncomfortable situation.*

Divide the students into small groups. Tell each group to discuss the answers written for the situations at the end of their *What You Have Learned* activity sheets. Group members should listen to each answer and, as a group, decide on one answer. Set a time limit. When the allotted time is up, have each group present its answers to the class.

Some possible answers are:

1. Not get upset

2. Find out the facts before reacting

3. Explain to him why it is important for you to watch the show. Maybe you can make a deal. For example, you might let him watch something special because he lets you watch your favorite show.

Have the students put their completed papers into their notebooks to save for their own personal future reference.

OPTIONAL SUGGESTION:

Arrange for the school social worker or counselor to come to the class or group to explain his/her job function. This will let the students know that there is a person in the school to whom they can go for help.

MANAGING ANGER

Modeling influences reactions to anger.

What is *anger*? *Anger* is a sudden violent feeling of displeasure with an impulse to retaliate. Everyone experiences anger at some point. Anger is a basic and primary emotion.

Anger is an emotion that is not generally trained or taught. However, your reactions to anger—your anger-management skills—are generally learned from *modeling.* Modeling is learned from the influential people you come into contact with or from your immediate surroundings. Modeling can demonstrate healthy or unhealthy ways of handling anger. The anger-management techniques you learn depend on the actions of your adult role-models, older siblings, and friends. Unfortunately, a great many role-models have unhealthy ways of handling anger and stress.

Develop good anger-management techniques.

Some people suppress or repress anger. This is not healthy. Some people explode in rage when something that angers them is said. This is not healthy, either. When attempting to develop good anger-management skills, you first need to be able to identify the behaviors that hurt you and hurt the people around you. If your anger-management skills are poor, you need to learn new ones. Research indicates that ineffective and inappropriate anger-management techniques can be changed and replaced with effective and appropriate techniques. Some of these effective and appropriate anger-management techniques are:

1. **When you talk with adult authority figures, think before you speak.** Weigh all of the consequences before saying something that might get you into trouble. Ask yourself, "Is it going to be worth it to talk back to my parent or teacher?" When talking, stay calm and in control. Say calmly, without interrupting, "Mom, can I explain what happened?" When you are calm, adults respond in a calmer manner. Remember: The only thing you gain by making smart comments is more trouble.

2. **Ignore the person who is annoying you.** Sometimes it's important to confront a person about a particular situation. Sometimes it's best to walk away and say it's not worth getting into trouble over. Consider the specifics of each situation. Remember: Some people know which buttons to push to make you angry. Remain calm. Then *you're* in control. The people who enjoy upsetting you know the key words that trigger negative responses from you. Most kids respond negatively by getting upset when someone makes fun of their parents, but when they respond to vague statements like "Your mama," they are making a poor choice of handling their anger. "Your mama" is a generic phrase that does not make a direct attack on anyone's mother.

3. **Count to 10 to calm yourself down and relax.** This gives you an opportunity to think things through.

4. **Use self-control.** Tell yourself that responding to the situation wouldn't be worth the aggravation. Remind yourself that a person thinks things through without re-

sorting to name-calling or physical confrontation. If you refuse to argue or fight, this leaves the other person with no one but him/herself to fight and argue with. This is a good way of handling the situation, because you are in control. Maintaining self-control should be your goal.

Change occurs only if you want it to.

Before change can take place, you must *want* it to happen. You must *want* to change your old behaviors for new ones. New behaviors can be forced upon you. But unless you are ready to change, they will not work. A doctor can tell a man that smoking is bad for his health, and that unless the man stops smoking, his habit will kill him. The man hears the doctor and understands what he says. But unless the patient is willing to stop smoking, the doctor's words are wasted.

Act smart in uncomfortable situations.

Most people experience conflict and anger. Conflict, if not resolved, can turn into anger. Children of divorce are often hurt when promises made to them are not kept. For example, if your father promises to pick you up at 7:00 and go for pizza and he stands you up, you have a right to tell him how you feel. Express your feelings honestly, but don't attack anyone verbally or physically. Remember: When your anger is legitimate, you have the right to tell the other person how you feel. When you are angry, you should:

1. attack the problem, not the person. Don't curse, call names, or hurt anyone in any way.

2. make every effort not to blame anyone, but be specific in identifying the problem.

3. listen to what the other person is saying. Don't interrupt while he/she is talking. When it is your turn, he/she should show you the same respect.

4. maintain good eye contact. People trust people who look directly at them.

5. use good body language. Do not stand with your arms folded, keep them at your sides. Don't frown or purse your lips. Don't stand with your head tilted to one side or your body leaning to one side.

6. try to see the problem from the other person's point of view. This is hard to do, but it is important.

7. ask questions. If you don't understand something, don't assume you know what the other person means. Remember: That person is standing in front of you, and this is a perfect opportunity to clear things up.

8. try not to raise your voice or yell. Yelling or shouting makes you angrier and puts the other person on the defensive.

9. use humor, if it's appropriate. Apologize, even if the mistake was not yours. Sometimes these techniques can diffuse an uncomfortable situation.

WHAT YOU HAVE LEARNED

Directions: Make a list of the ways people act when they're angry. It may help to think of how you or someone you know acts when upset.

When people are angry, they might:

1. _____
2. _____
3. _____
4. _____
5. _____
6. _____
7. _____
8. _____
9. _____
10. _____
11. _____
12. _____
13. _____
14. _____

Directions: Make a list of appropriate ways of expressing your anger. Use words or actions that will not hurt or belittle another person.

1. _____
2. _____
3. _____
4. _____
5. _____
6. _____
7. _____
8. _____
9. _____

Read the following situations. Each one could make you angry. What anger-management skills could you use to resolve each situation peaceably? Write your answers in the space provided.

1. A boy with thick glasses bumps into you and accidentally knocks books out of your arms. How would you resolve this situation peaceably?

2. You overhear a boy refer to Mary as a "fat cow." You get very upset and you are about to rush over to him in anger. Mary is your mother's name, and your mother is heavy, so you assume he's talking about your mother. How would you resolve this situation peaceably?

3. You want to watch TV because a special program is coming on. Your brother is using the TV to play video games. How do you resolve this situation peaceably?

13

NEGATIVE BEHAVIORS I NEED TO WORK ON
(LEADER'S GUIDE)

MATERIALS NEEDED:

For each student:

- Copy of *Negative Behaviors I Need to Work on* (pages 58-59)
- Pencil

For the leader:

- Extra copies of *Negative Behaviors I Need to Work on* (pages 58-59)

LESSON:

Tell the students:

In order to make improvements in your lives, you need to be aware of your negative behaviors. The purpose of this lesson is to help you identify your negative behaviors by making an inventory. Understand that an inventory has no right or wrong answers. It is not a test, but a survey. It is a preventive measure to ensure that you maintain a healthy attitude. Everyone has behaviors that need improving, and admitting to having shortcomings and weaknesses does not make you—or anyone else—weak.

Distribute a copy of the reproduced materials (pages 58-59) and a pencil to each student. Tell the students to read *Negative Behaviors I Need to Work on* and follow the directions to complete the *Negative Behavior Inventory*. Set a time limit for this activity.

When the allotted time is up, discuss the students' answers. Some students may be reluctant to share their shortcomings with the group. If this happens, remind them that admitting shortcomings is not a sign of weakness, but a sign of strength. If there is still little cooperation, ask the students to write on a piece of paper the number for each behavior they have checked. Collect the papers and tally the responses. If several students checked similar boxes, consider this an indication to the counselor, social worker, or teacher that these students could benefit from participating in a small group to work on developing more positive skills.

Tell the students who indicated that they would like to work with someone to make changes to make an appointment for an individual conference with the person of their choice.

Distribute extra copies of the *Negative Behaviors I Need to Work on* to students who wish to have another person complete the inventory about them.

Have the students put their completed papers into their notebooks to save for their own personal future reference.

NEGATIVE BEHAVIORS I NEED TO WORK ON

An inventory is not a test. It is a survey. There are no right or wrong answers to an inventory. Its purpose is to help you see how many negative behaviors you have and what you need to work on in order to improve the quality of your life.

Everyone has behaviors that need improving. Taking an inventory, on occasion, is a preventive measure to ensure that you maintain a healthy attitude. It's kind of like going to a doctor for a checkup to make sure your body is in good condition.

When you take the inventory, it is important to understand that admitting to having shortcomings and weaknesses does not make you a weak person. All of us have strengths and weaknesses. Once you know what your strengths and weaknesses are, you can either work hard to change your weaknesses or focus on your strengths and make them stronger. The choice is yours.

NEGATIVE BEHAVIOR INVENTORY

Directions: Put a check (✓) in front of each thing you have done or thought about doing during the past week. Remember: Being aware of your behaviors will help you know what you need to improve.

- [ ] 1. called someone a name in order to hurt him/her
- [ ] 2. pretended to understand the instructions for how to do an assignment instead of asking for help
- [ ] 3. felt I was right and that my way was the only way
- [ ] 4. made someone feel alone or wrong by not supporting him/her
- [ ] 5. wanted to have my own way most of the time
- [ ] 6. argued frequently
- [ ] 7. blamed others for things I had done
- [ ] 8. lied about someone
- [ ] 9. interrupted someone while he/she was talking, or did not listen while someone was talking

☐ 10. refused to answer someone because I was afraid I would say or do the wrong thing, I just didn't like the person, or I was afraid I would draw attention to myself

☐ 11. picked fights with other students. This includes tripping, throwing objects at people, annoying them in other ways

Go back and reread the statements next to the boxes you have checked.

Are there any behaviors that you would like to change?

Would you be willing to work with your counselor or teacher to change some of your negative behaviors?

Are you really brave? If you really feel brave and confident, ask the teacher for another copy of this inventory and have another student—or your counselor, teacher, or parent—complete the survey about you. Then check your list against his/hers.

|14|
ALTERNATIVES TO FIGHTING
(LEADER'S GUIDE)

MATERIALS NEEDED:

For each student:

- Copy of *Alternatives to Fighting* (page 61)
- Pencil

For each student group:

- Copy of *Role-Play* (pages 62-63)

LESSON:

Tell the students:

> The purpose of this lesson is help you to learn safe ways to release anger. Some suggestions are: communicating, talking about uncomfortable situations with someone you trust, learning to develop hobbies and interests, telling the person you're angry with that you're too upset to talk, and walking away. You can also join a school group, church, or community club.

Distribute a copy of the reproduced material (page 61) and a pencil to each student. Tell the students to read *Alternatives to Fighting* and follow the directions in the *What You Have Learned* section. Set a time limit for this activity. When the allotted time is up, ask the students to share their suggestions.

Divide the students into two groups. Give each group a copy of *Role-Play* (pages 62-63). Tell the students to read both role-plays, select students from within their groups to be the characters, and practice each role-play. Tell the students to be sure to include a safe solution. When the group members have finished their presentation, the other members of the group are to critique the role-play and offer additional solutions. Set a time limit for this activity. If time permits, the group may think of other uncomfortable situations and role-play them, using a safe solution for each one.

When the allotted time is up, have each group select one role-play to perform for the class. Have the class react to each group's role-play.

Have the students put their completed papers into their notebooks to save for their own personal future reference.

ALTERNATIVES TO FIGHTING

Everyone gets angry. What is important is that you do not let your anger cause you to get into trouble.

The following suggestions are alternatives to violence and fighting.

1. *Communicating* is one alternative to fighting and violence. This means talking with someone you trust about your anger. Don't be afraid to ask for help.

2. Write in a journal about how you feel.

3. Draw a picture to express your feelings, solve your problem, or just relax.

4. Do something you enjoy.

5. Develop a hobby.

6. Tell the other person you're too upset to talk, then walk away. When you're upset, it can be easy to say something you will later regret.

7. Join a school group, church, or community club.

WHAT YOU HAVE LEARNED

Directions: Think of other safe ways to release anger. Name two community, church, or school clubs that could offer you an alternative to gang membership.

1. _____
2. _____

Directions: See if you can think of other safe ways to release anger. Name two interests or hobbies that could be alternatives to fighting.

1. _____
2. _____

Directions: See if you can think of other safe ways to release anger. Name two people you feel you can talk with when you're angry and ready to fight.

1. _____
2. _____

ROLE-PLAY

Directions: Read the descriptions below. Select students from your group to role-play the situations. Tell the students doing the role-play to act out the situation and include a safe solution to the problem. When they have finished their presentation, critique the role-play and discuss other alternative solutions for the problem. If time permits, write descriptions of other uncomfortable situations that could make a person angry, then act them out. When the time allotted for this activity has elapsed, select one role-play from the two presented here—or original ones thought up by the group—and enact it for the class.

1. Tom, a student in your class, has been bothering you. You talk with the teacher. She tells Tom to sit in the seat of a student who is absent that day. When Tom returns to his desk to get his books, he whispers annoying things to you. What do you do?

2. You and two friends are upset because three tough boys behind you are talking so loudly that you can't enjoy the movie you paid $7.00 to see. The boys behind you are yelling at the actors on the screen, telling them what to do. Everyone is annoyed by the disturbance, but too afraid to do anything. What should you do?

OTHER SITUATIONS

ANGER ALTERNATIVES
(LEADER'S GUIDE)

MATERIALS NEEDED:

For each student:

- Copy of *Anger Alternatives* (page 67)

LESSON:

Tell the students:

> The purpose of this lesson is to help you understand the necessity of having alternative actions to use in situations that make you angry. Anger alternatives can prevent you from getting into trouble and can help you develop good coping skills. They can help you stay in control. Remember: When you are angry, don't attack the *person*. Attack the *problem* that is causing the conflict.

Distribute a copy of the reproduced material (page 67) to each student. Have the students form pairs. Tell the students:

> Listen as I read each *Anger Alternative*. Then read the situation on your paper that matches it. Talk with your partner about how the *Anger Alternative* could be used in this situation.

Read the following *Anger Alternatives:*

Anger Alternative #1: Chill or take a "Time Out."

> This means don't get angry. Or if your anger cannot be controlled, remove yourself from the person(s) causing the anger. Read the situation described under this alternative. Discuss it with your partner for two or three minutes, then be ready to share your thoughts with the class.

Anger Alternative #2: Walk away before you explode or before name-calling begins.

> It's difficult not to retaliate when someone calls you a name or accuses you of something you didn't do, but staying in the situation will only make it worse. Read the situation described under this alternative. Discuss it with your partner for two or three minutes, then be ready to share your thoughts with the class.

Anger Alternative #3: Talk with someone you trust.

All of us have had experiences in which we have trusted the wrong person. Think about whom you could trust in the situation below and discuss with your partner why you chose that person. Discuss this for two or three minutes, then be ready to share your thoughts with the class.

Anger Alternative #4: Exercise or do something physical to release energy and anger.

Sometimes your feelings are so strong that you want to strike out at someone and you almost lose control. Those feelings aren't going to go away by themselves. Read the situation described below and discuss with your partner what you would do to release your angry energy. Discuss this for two or three minutes, then be ready to share your thoughts with the class.

Anger Alternative #5: Do breathing exercises to help you relax.

There are different breathing exercises you can use to help you relax. One is to breathe in deeply through your nose to a slow count of 10. Then exhale through your mouth to a slow count of 10. Breathing exercises have a calming effect and can settle you down when your angry feelings threaten to cause you to lose control. Read the situation described under this alternative. Discuss it with your partner for two or three minutes, then be ready to share your thoughts with the class.

Anger Alternative #6: Cry, if you need to.

Sometimes you can be so angry that crying is a way of releasing the anger. Read the situation described under this alternative. Discuss it with your partner for two or three minutes, then be ready to share your thoughts with the class.

Explain to the students that they will be doing two different role-plays. Tell the students that you will read the first role-play aloud and then choose one or more teams of students to act out the situation using the *Anger Alternatives* that have just been studied.

Role-Play #1: It is June 15, and you are an eighth-grade student preparing to graduate. The school principal informs you two days prior to graduation that you won't be able to graduate because your reading score is too low. You have a 7.9 reading score, and the Board of Education mandates that you have an 8.0 reading score to graduate. When your mother comes to school to talk with the principal, she is angry.

Select three students to participate in the role-play. Assign one to be the angry eighth-grade student, one to be the principal, and one to be the angry parent. If more than one team of role-players is desired, continue selecting groups of three until you have as many groups as you want. Allow time for the students to practice. Then have the group(s) present their role-play(s). After each role-play, discuss the presentation.

Role-Play #2: You are a high school senior. Your younger brother, who is in the fourth grade, steals your $100.00 gold necklace and sells it to another student for $5.00. You go to school to get it back. When you arrive, you go directly to your brother's classroom.

Select three students to participate in the role-play. Assign one student to be the fourth-grade student, one to be the teacher, and one to be the older sibling (boy or girl). If more than one team of role-players is desired, continue selecting groups of three until you have as many groups as you want. Allow time for the students to practice. Then have the group(s) present their role-play(s). After each role-play, discuss the presentation.

Have the students put their papers into their notebooks to save for their own personal future reference.

ANGER ALTERNATIVES

We will begin by discussing some things you can do that will allow you to remain in control and keep you from getting into trouble when you are angry. Pair up with another student. As each *Anger Alternative* is mentioned, read the scenario described below it and discuss with your partner how this *Anger Alternative* could be used in this situation.

Chill or take a "Time Out."

Your parents have just informed you that you are going to baby-sit your younger brother tonight. You and your best friends had been planning for a week to go to the movies tonight. This is the last night the movie you want to see will be playing.

Walk away before you explode or before name-calling begins.

Another student has called you a sloppy, fat liar and accused you of cheating on your math test.

Talk with someone you trust.

You tell a friend whom you trust that you spent the $40.00 your mother gave you to pay for school books on a girl (or boy) you met last week. Now the girl (boy) has dumped you. Your friend tells another friend, who tells his mother. She is your mother's best friend!

Exercise or do something physical to release energy and anger.

Your girlfriend (or boyfriend) bought you a special box of candy, and your younger brother ate all of it. You were just about to hit him when your mother came into the room and stopped you.

Do breathing exercises to relax.

You were just in a fight, and your teacher says you might be suspended for three days. Your parents have told you that if you got into any more trouble at school, they would send you to live with an uncle whom you hate.

Cry, if you need to.

You learn that your best friend has been in an accident and is in critical condition.

CONFLICT-RESOLUTION

| 16 |
What is Conflict?

| 17 |
Choices! Choices! Choices!

| 18 |
Fight Fairly in Conflict Situations

16
WHAT IS CONFLICT?
(LEADER'S GUIDE)

MATERIALS NEEDED:

For each student:

- Copy of *What is Conflict?* (pages 71-72)
- Pencil

LESSON:

Tell the students:

> The purpose of this lesson is to help you understand that conflict is, and always will be, a natural part of our everyday lives. Conflict can range from a simple argument to a horrendous war. Conflicts are not always bad. They sometimes bring about change, and when they do that, they can be helpful. It is important to remember that there are always at least two sides to any conflict. Conflict can often be resolved nonviolently. But sometimes, in the case of a war, this is not so and violent actions occur.

Distribute a copy of the reproduced materials (pages 71-72) and a pencil to each student. Tell the students to read *What is Conflict?* and then complete the *What You Have Learned* section. Set a time limit for this activity.

When the allotted time is up, have the students discuss their answers with the class. There are no specific right or wrong answers to the questions, and any appropriate answer should be accepted.

Have the students put their completed papers into their notebooks to save for their own personal future reference.

WHAT IS CONFLICT?

Conflict does not necessarily involve violence.

Conflict is defined as a disagreement, quarrel, or controversy. It is a natural part of our lives. Violence is *not* natural! Violence occurs when someone tries to hurt someone else.

Conflict can range from a simple argument to a horrendous war.

There are always at least two sides in a conflict, and each side thinks that it's right. When we argue with our friends or parents, we are involved in a conflict but not in an act of violence. These arguments are not necessarily bad. Conflicts can be helpful, and they can bring about change. For example, public and political debates are a form of conflict that represents an effort to bring about change. War is something different. Both parties in a war want to bring about change, but the parties involved hurt people in the process. War can be a conflict between nations or groups of people who see things differently. Many television talk shows feature conflict, but most of it is nonviolent.

Most conflicts can be resolved nonviolently.

In any conflict situation, there are always at least two sides. Conflicts, if handled properly, can usually be resolved nonviolently. Unfortunately, when people do not handle conflicts properly, they sometimes become violent.

There are three types of conflict.

There are essentially three types of conflict:

1. **Internal Conflict.** We all have internal struggles or conflicts. An example of an internal conflict might occur when it is necessary to make a decision between playing a video game or studying for a test scheduled for the next day.

2. **External Conflicts Between People.** These are disagreements between children or adults. A conflict between classmates could be as simple as who got to the drinking fountain first or as violent as an after-school fight.

3. **External Conflicts Between Nations or Groups of People.** These conflicts can be as simple as a conflict over whether a politician will support a bill being brought to a vote in Congress or as violent as union members attacking workers crossing a picket line.

WHAT YOU HAVE LEARNED

1. **Internal conflicts involve only one person—yourself.** We all have internal struggles or conflicts.

   Name two internal conflicts you have recently experienced:

   1.

   2.

2. **External conflicts occur between people.** External conflicts are fights or arguments between children or adults.

   Describe two external conflicts in which you were recently involved:

   1.

   2.

3. **External conflicts can occur between nations or between groups of people.**

   Name two types of conflicts that have occurred between groups or between nations:

   1.

   2.

17
CHOICES! CHOICES! CHOICES!
(LEADER'S GUIDE)

MATERIALS NEEDED:

For each student:

- Copy of *Choices! Choices! Choices!* (pages 75-77)
- Pencil

LESSON:

Tell the students:

> You make choices every day—in school, at home, and in the community. The purpose of this lesson is to help you understand that as you get older, you will have more and more choices to make. Sometimes you will be confronted with internal conflicts. These are conflicts that involve only yourself, knowing right from wrong, and making the best choice. Sometimes there will be conflicts between you and other people. If you have good self-esteem, you will be able to make better choices and better decisions.

Distribute a copy of the reproduced materials (pages 75-77) and a pencil to each student. Tell the students to read *Choices! Choices! Choices!* and then complete the *What You Have Learned* section. Set a time limit for this activity. When the allotted time is up, have the students share their answers to the questions. The answers may be varied, and you should accept any reasonable answer.

Have the students put their completed papers into their notebooks to save for their own personal future reference.

OPTIONAL ACTIVITY:

Make a list of things that are different from one another, such as: robin–eagle, quiet–noisy, peanut butter–spaghetti, etc. Divide the room into two sides. Read each combination on the list, designate a side for each word, and have each student go to the side of the room that fits him/her best. To extend the activity, make a list of three-item and four-item sets. For example: black–white–gray, penny–quarter–dollar, or spring–summer–autumn–fall.

CHOICES! CHOICES! CHOICES!

Your memory bank stores the consequences of your behavior.

When you were younger, most decisions were made for you. But as you get older, you will be expected to make more and more choices for yourself. Each situation you encountered as a child has become part of your memory bank. This is where you have stored behavior and consequences, much like a computer stores information. When a similar situation occurs, you remember what you did the last time and what the consequences of your actions were.

Everyone is confronted by internal conflicts that require decisions.

> Should I be on time for class or hang out on the corner with my friends and be late?

> Mom left her CD player on the kitchen table. Should I leave it there or take it to school? (You remember that she told you not to use it. But since you'll get home before she does, she'll never know.)

Once your mind grasps the situation, it runs through all the possible consequences. For instance, you might drop or lose the CD player at school, the teacher might confiscate it, or it might get stolen from your bookbag or locker. If any one of these situations occurs, there will be a *conflict* between you and your mother. When you face new and challenging situations, your mind refers your memory bank to similar situations you faced in the past and, based upon your knowledge of right from wrong and your conscience, you make the best decisions possible in the present situation.

Skill and knowledge contribute to decision-making.

You use your skill and knowledge to make good decisions about what clothes to wear to school. You make a decision based on school code, what clothes you have, and what's appropriate for the weather. This is why you wake up and decide not to wear shorts and sandals to school when there is snow on the ground.

You make choices all day every day—in school, at home, and in the community. For instance, when the teacher asks you to stop talking, but you choose to continue talking, you make a decision based on the choice to stop or continue, realizing there will be consequences if you continue talking.

Self-esteem influences decision-making.

Self-esteem is important. If you have good self-esteem, you will be able to make better choices and decisions.

Think things through before making a decision.

In order to make better decisions, you need to know:

- the choices involved

- all the information about the situation

- the risks involved: "If I do this, these will be the consequences. Is it worth it? Do I want to be in trouble?"

- how the choices make you feel

- which choice will be better for you.

WHAT YOU HAVE LEARNED

Directions: List five rules you have in your school or classroom. Then tell whether you follow each rule.

Do you follow the rule?

1. _____ ☐ YES ☐ NO ☐ SOMETIMES
2. _____ ☐ YES ☐ NO ☐ SOMETIMES
3. _____ ☐ YES ☐ NO ☐ SOMETIMES
4. _____ ☐ YES ☐ NO ☐ SOMETIMES
5. _____ ☐ YES ☐ NO ☐ SOMETIMES

Directions: List five rules you have in your home. Then tell whether you follow each rule.

Do you follow the rule?

1. _____ ☐ YES ☐ NO ☐ SOMETIMES
2. _____ ☐ YES ☐ NO ☐ SOMETIMES
3. _____ ☐ YES ☐ NO ☐ SOMETIMES
4. _____ ☐ YES ☐ NO ☐ SOMETIMES
5. _____ ☐ YES ☐ NO ☐ SOMETIMES

Directions: List five rules you have in your community. Then tell whether you follow each rule.

Do you follow the rule?

1. _____ ☐ YES ☐ NO ☐ SOMETIMES
2. _____ ☐ YES ☐ NO ☐ SOMETIMES
3. _____ ☐ YES ☐ NO ☐ SOMETIMES
4. _____ ☐ YES ☐ NO ☐ SOMETIMES
5. _____ ☐ YES ☐ NO ☐ SOMETIMES

Directions: List five decisions you make often. Then describe the other choices you could make in each situation.

1. Decision: _____

   Choices: _____

   _____

2. Decision: _____

   Choices: _____

   _____

3. Decision: _____

   Choices: _____

   _____

4. Decision: _____

   Choices: _____

   _____

5. Decision: _____

   Choices: _____

   _____

18
FIGHT FAIRLY IN CONFLICT SITUATIONS
(LEADER'S GUIDE)

MATERIALS NEEDED:

For each student:

- Copy of *Fight Fairly in Conflict Situations* (pages 79-80)
- Pencil

For each student group:

- Newspaper articles describing conflicts (If you wish, the students may be asked to bring these articles to the class.)

LESSON:

Tell the students:

> The purpose of this lesson is to help you understand that conflicts are a natural part of our lives because people see things differently. Whenever there is more than one person, there is a possibility of more than one version of any incident. It is not uncommon for two people to look at the same object and see it very differently. There are three different types of conflict: internal conflicts, conflicts with another person, and conflicts that occur between groups or nations. Conflicts are here to stay, and it is important to learn to deal with them fairly. When dealt with fairly, conflicts can be positive, rather than negative, occurrences.

Distribute a copy of the reproduced materials (pages 79-80) and a pencil to each student. Tell the students to read *Fight Fairly in Conflict Situations* and then complete the *What You Have Learned* section. Set a time limit for this activity. When the allotted time is up, have the students share their answers. The answers may be varied, and you should accept any reasonable answer.

Divide the students into small groups of three to five members. Distribute the newspaper articles. Have the groups discuss the conflicts the articles describe, telling how each conflict could have been settled if the people involved had acted fairly. Resume the class and have each group share its findings with the rest of the students.

Have the students put their completed papers into their notebooks to save for their own personal future reference.

FIGHT FAIRLY IN CONFLICT SITUATIONS

Expect conflicts in your life.

Whenever more than one person has an opinion about a situation, there is a possibility of conflict. People can look at the same object and see it very differently. Remember the story about two people looking at a glass of water? One thought it was half-full, the other thought it was half-empty.

Conflicts are a natural part of life. They have always been with us, and they will always be a part of our lives. Conflicts in themselves are not bad. They become bad when they are not dealt with fairly.

Resolve conflicts fairly.

Follow these rules for learning to resolve conflicts in a fair manner:

1. Identify the problem. Know what it really is, not what you *think* it is.
2. Concentrate on the *problem*, not the *person*.
3. Don't attack the *person*, attack the *problem* causing the conflict. Make sure you know everything you need to know before making a judgment.
4. Listen with an open mind to the other person.
5. Admit when you're wrong.
6. Benefit from your mistakes. Learn from them so you won't make the same mistakes again.

WHAT YOU HAVE LEARNED

Complete the following:

1. Think of an internal conflict you have experienced. Describe the problem as it really was—not as you *thought* it was.

   Internal conflict:

   Problem:

2. Think of an external conflict you were involved in recently. Describe the conflict, your side of the argument, the other person's side of the argument, and how it could have been resolved fairly.

External conflict:

My side:

The other person's side:

Fair resolution:

SAFE SURROUNDINGS

|19|
Safe Places and People

|20|
What Makes a Home Safe?

|21|
Safe Neighborhoods

|22|
School as a Safe Place

|23|
Everyone and Everything
Has a Right to Live

19

SAFE PLACES AND PEOPLE
(LEADER'S GUIDE)

MATERIALS NEEDED:

For each student:

- Copy of *Safe Places and People* (pages 83-85)
- Pencil

LESSON:

Tell the students:

> The purpose of this lesson is to help you understand that being aware of people, places, and things that are safe not only protects you against violence but can save your life. *Safety awareness* means learning to protect yourself against violence. Safety awareness begins by learning to recognize safe places in your community and learning how to become aware of safe places wherever you go. Knowing people who are safe will also protect you from danger and harm. Knowing what people, places, and things are safe means knowing what people, places, and things are *not* safe.

Distribute a copy of the reproduced materials (pages 83-85) and a pencil to each student. Tell the students to read *Safe Places and People,* then complete the *What You Have Learned* section. Set a time limit for this activity. When the allotted time is up, have the students share their answers. The questions are subjective, and all answers should be accepted.

Have the students put their completed papers into their notebooks to save for their own personal future reference.

SAFE PLACES AND PEOPLE

What is *safety awareness?*

Safety awareness is the process of learning to protect yourself against violence. Start by learning to recognize the safe places in your community and becoming aware of safe places wherever you go.

Safety awareness also means being able to openly and honestly express and discuss your feelings about fear and violence. Sometimes, having fears can be good for you. Sometimes, being afraid can save your life.

Know your community.

If you live in an unsafe neighborhood, you need to know what people and what places to avoid in order to keep yourself safe. Becoming alert about where you live could save your life.

Know the good guys and avoid the bad guys in your community and at school. Know where gang hangouts and drug houses are located and stay away from them. A good rule to remember is that vacant, boarded-up buildings and burnt-out buildings are *always* unsafe and dangerous places to play. They are often spots where drug addicts and gang members meet.

If your neighborhood is plagued with graffiti-covered buildings, gangs, poor housing, truancy, illiteracy, and unemployment, you live in a troubled area and your fear is realistic. It may even help you find some ways to turn your troubled neighborhood around by making use of assets and resources.

Safe places include YMCAs, Boys and Girls Clubs, neighborhood centers, church activities, and supervised after-school sports and recreation programs.

WHAT YOU HAVE LEARNED

Directions: Check the box that applies to each of the places or people below. If anything on the list does not apply to you, leave it blank.

	SAFE	UNSAFE
1. Home	☐	☐
2. School	☐	☐
3. Church	☐	☐
4. School bus	☐	☐
5. Police station	☐	☐
6. Relative's home (Name: _____)	☐	☐
7. Community Center	☐	☐
8. Parents	☐	☐
9. Sisters/Brothers	☐	☐
10. Baby Sitter	☐	☐

Directions: Complete the following sentences.

1. The person I feel closest to is _____.

2. The person I feel closest to makes me feel special because _____
   _____.

3. My three best friends are _____
   _____.

4. I like my friends because _____
   _____.

5. The person I can talk with when I am sad or unhappy is _____.

6. The person I trust more than anyone in the world is _____.

7. The place where I feel most safe is _____.

List some of the resources in your community that could be used to help make your community a better place to live.

1201
WHAT MAKES A HOME SAFE?
(LEADER'S GUIDE)

MATERIALS NEEDED:

For each student:

- Copy of *What Makes a Home Safe?* (pages 87-89)
- Pencil

LESSON:

Tell the students:

> The purpose of this lesson is to point out some factors that can make a home unsafe. Then, thinking about these factors, you will evaluate the safety of your own home.

Distribute a copy of the reproduced materials (pages 87-89) and a pencil to each student. Have the students read the information in *What Makes a Home Safe?* then complete the questionnaire in the What *You Have Learned* section. Set a time limit for this activity. When the allotted time is up, have the students share their answers. The topics are subjective, and any appropriate answer should be accepted.

Have the students put their completed papers into their notebooks to save for their own personal future reference.

WHAT MAKES A HOME SAFE?

Many homes today have guns.

There are many reasons why people keep guns in their homes. Some families use them for hunting. Others use guns for protection. Some people collect them. Do you have one or more guns in your home?

Many parents hide guns from their children or lock them up. They do this to avoid the risk of having their children find a gun and accidentally hurt someone or commit a crime. If there are guns in a home, what should parents do to make that home as safe as possible?

Some parents are alcoholics and/or drug abusers.

In some homes, parents drink heavily and use drugs. Do you believe a child would feel safe in a home where this type of behavior occurs? Children who live in homes where this type of behavior occurs may need to seek advice from a counselor or organization that specializes in helping children from alcoholic and drug-abusing families.

WHAT YOU HAVE LEARNED

Read each sentence. Complete each sentence by using the name of a person/thing that best fits the description.

1. The person at home who makes me feel really comfortable is _____.

2. The person at home whom I trust most is _____.

3. A person at home who is special is _____.

4. At home, I feel I can always count on _____ to be there for me.

5. If I could change one rule at home, it would be _____
   _____.

6. If I were a parent, I would tell my child to _____
   _____.

7. The room at home where I feel safest is _____.

8. My parents set rules at home in order to _____
   _____.

9. A rule we need at home is _____
   _____.

10. When I have children, the rules I will expect my kids to follow are _____
    _____
    _____
    _____.

11. The most important rule in my house is _____
   _____.

12. When I'm away from home, I still follow the rules my parents taught me. Those rules are:

   _____
   _____
   _____.

13. Strange or new places make me feel _____
   _____.

14. My family is _____
   _____.

15. I feel embarrassed when my family _____
   _____
   _____.

16. If I could be a member of a TV family, it would be the _____.

17. I wish I could do _____
   to make my mother or father happy.

On a scale of 1 (very unsafe) to 10 (very safe), I would rank my home:

1.....2.....3.....4.....5.....6.....7.....8.....9.....10

VERY UNSAFE **SAFE**

21

SAFE NEIGHBORHOODS
(LEADER'S GUIDE)

Note: If Lesson 19 has already been presented, this lesson can be used as a review or omitted entirely.

MATERIALS NEEDED:

For each student:

- Copy of *Safe Neighborhoods* (pages 91-93)
- Black, red, and blue crayon
- Pencil

LESSON:

Tell the students:

> The purpose of this lesson is to teach you how to identify safe places in your neighborhood. Knowing where to find safe places will keep you safe. It can protect you against violence and can even save your life. You need to know what people and places to avoid in order to stay safe. Remember: Even some places and people that appear to be safe can actually be dangerous.

Distribute a copy of the reproduced materials (pages 91-93) and crayons to each student. Tell the students to read *Safe Neighborhoods,* draw a map of their neighborhood, and complete the chart under the *What You Have Learned* section. Set a time limit for this activity. When the allotted time is up, have the students share their answers from the *What You Have Learned* section and their maps.

Have the students put their completed papers into their notebooks to save for their own personal future reference.

SAFE NEIGHBORHOODS

Recognize the safe places in your neighborhood.

Safety awareness is the process of learning to protect yourself against violence. Safety awareness begins by learning to recognize the safe places in your neighborhood and becoming aware of safe places wherever you go.

Safety awareness also means being able to openly and honestly express and discuss your feelings about fear and violence.

Being fearful can be smart.

Sometimes it is smart to have fears. If you live in an unsafe neighborhood, you need to know what people and places to avoid to keep yourself safe. You need to know who the good guys are and how to avoid the bad guys. You can avoid gang hangouts and drug houses if you know where they are. Vacant and burnt-out buildings are *always* unsafe and dangerous places to go. Vacant, boarded-up buildings are often spots where drug addicts and gang members hang out.

Know and go to safe places.

Safe places include YMCAs, Boys and Girls Clubs, neighborhood centers, church activities, after-school sports and clubs, and supervised recreation programs.

MAP

Draw a map showing where you live and the area within several miles of your home. Be sure to include the various buildings within that area.

WHAT YOU HAVE LEARNED

Look at your map. Put a red "X" on each of the unsafe places, a black "X" on each of the safe places, and a blue circle around those buildings that are sometimes safe and sometimes unsafe.

Complete the following by listing all the safe places you marked on the map under the correct heading. Do the same with the other two headings. Then, if you can think of more places, add them to the appropriate list.

SAFE PLACES	UNSAFE PLACES	SOMETIMES SAFE/ SOMETIMES UNSAFE
_____	_____	_____
_____	_____	_____
_____	_____	_____
_____	_____	_____
_____	_____	_____
_____	_____	_____
_____	_____	_____
_____	_____	_____
_____	_____	_____

1221
SCHOOL AS A SAFE PLACE
(LEADER'S GUIDE)

MATERIALS NEEDED:

For each student:

- Copy of *School as a Safe Place* (pages 96-97)
- Pencil
- 3 slips of paper

LESSON:

Tell the students:

> The purpose of this lesson is to help you understand that school should be a safety zone where you can feel safe and secure. You will complete a questionnaire that will allow you to give your opinion about the safety of your school.

Distribute a copy of the reproduced materials (pages 96-97) and a pencil to each student. Tell the students to complete the unfinished sentences in the *What You Have Learned* section. Set a time limit for this activity. When the allotted time is up, have the students share their answers. Because the questions are all based on personal experiences and are subjective, the students' answers will vary. Accept all appropriate answers.

Distribute three slips of paper to each student. Tell the students there is going to be a secret vote about their feelings related to school safety. Explain that questions will be asked and that they are to answer them on the slips of paper. Assure the students that no one will know how they answer the questions. Then say:

> List the three most unsafe places in this school. Number them one, two, and three.

Then ask:

> Are gangs a problem in this school?
>
> What do you most fear happening in school?

After the students have answered each question, collect the slips of paper. After the papers have been collected, ask a student to go to the chalkboard to tally the results of the first list.

Read the results to the class.

1. For question one, tell the student at the chalkboard to make three marks for every unsafe place numbered 1, two marks for every unsafe place numbered 2, and one mark for every unsafe place numbered 3. Read the three choices on each slip. Have the student write the name of the unsafe place and make marks after it. When all the votes have been read, tally the marks.

2. For question two, have another student go to the chalkboard. Do not erase the results of the first question. Have this student make two columns and label them "Yes" and "No." Read each result and tell the student to place a mark in the appropriate column. Tally the results after all the votes have been read.

3. For question three, select a third student to go to the chalkboard. Do not erase the previous results. Read the answers to this question and have the student write them on the chalkboard. Identify repeats by making a mark after the answer. Tally the results after all the answers have been read.

Ask the students to look at the results on the chalkboard. Then have each student orally rate the safety of the school on a scale of 1 (low risk) to 10 (high risk).

Have the students put their completed papers into their notebooks to save for their own personal future reference.

SCHOOL AS A SAFE PLACE
WHAT YOU HAVE LEARNED

Directions: School should be a safety zone for students. Complete the following sentences as they relate to your school and your feelings about its safety.

1. The person at school whom I trust most is _____.

2. A person at school who is special is _____.

3. When I have a problem at school, the person who is there for me is _____.

4. If I could change one rule at school, it would be _____.

5. If I were the teacher, I would tell my students _____.

6. The best part of school is _____.

7. My teacher sets rules in my class because _____.

8. One rule we need in our class is _____.

9. The most important rule in my class is _____
   _____.

10. Even when the teacher isn't looking, I follow the rules because _____
    _____.

11. When the teacher leaves the room or is not watching me, I feel _____
    _____.

12. My classroom is a _____ place.

13. My teacher makes me so angry when she/he _____
    _____.

14. Sometimes I get so angry inside that I feel like _____
    _____.

15. The hardest thing for me in school is _____
    and I feel _____ when I have to do it.

16. Students should not bring guns to school because _____ ,
    _____.

1231
EVERYONE AND EVERYTHING HAS A RIGHT TO LIVE
(LEADER'S GUIDE)

MATERIALS NEEDED:

For each student:

- Copy of *Everyone and Everything Has a Right to Live* (pages 99-100)
- Pencil

LESSON:

Tell the students:

> The purpose of this lesson is to help you understand that everything and everyone has a right to live and that only unhappy, angry people needlessly hurt animals or other people. No one has the right to take the life of another person unless his/her *own* life is in danger. Protecting one's self against violence or the threat of violence is called *self-defense*.

Distribute a copy of the reproduced materials (pages 99-100) and a pencil to each student. Tell the students to read *Everyone and Everything Has a Right to Live* and complete the *What You Have Learned* section. Set a time limit for this activity. When the allotted time is up, have the students share their answers. (Be alert for a "Yes" answer to questions #4 and #5.) The questions are subjective, and any appropriate answer should be accepted.

Have the students put their completed papers into their notebooks to save for their own personal future reference.

OPTIONAL ACTIVITY:

Ask the students to bring in pictures of family members and pets to share with the class. Have each student share one picture and tell the class how he/she would feel if someone injured his/her pet or someone he/she loved. When everyone has had a chance to share, have the class discuss the following questions:

> What type of person would hurt someone else?

> Why doesn't anyone have the right to hurt another living thing?

EVERYONE AND EVERYTHING HAS A RIGHT TO LIVE

Lives end in various ways.

Suicide is the act of deliberately taking one's own life. Suicide is against the law and violates most religions' teachings. People who attempt suicide are very unhappy people who need help. *Homicide* is the killing of one human being by another. *Murder* is the unlawful killing of a human being with malice aforethought.

It's hard to imagine someone wanting to end his/her own life or the life of another person, even under the worst of circumstances. Yet every day on the news, we hear about violent deaths, children killing other children, children and adults preying on the elderly, and spousal abuse that ends in death.

Unresolved conflicts can turn violent.

We know that conflict is a natural part of life. We also know that conflict, left unresolved, can turn violent. For this reason, any conflict needs to be addressed as quickly and as peaceably as possible. In order to accomplish this, the conflicting parties must have pro-social skills.

Life is sacred.

The only exception to the sanctity of another person's life is when *your* life is in danger and you are defending yourself from attack. In such a situation, violent action can be justified. But this is the exception, not the rule. The rule is that no one has the right to take the life of another person.

To some people, life is unimportant. These people feel no remorse when they deliberately hurt or kill another person. Fortunately, these people are outnumbered by those who value life.

Pets—like domestic dogs and cats—depend on their owners to feed and protect them. Yet we hear stories of children harming defenseless animals or house pets. Babies, too, are dependent and defenseless. They rely on their parents for love, pampering, protection, clothes, and food. Yet we hear reports of children being physically abused by parents and other adults. The sick and elderly depend on others for love, protection, and care. Yet we hear stories about the treatment they receive at the hands of relatives and caregivers. Hopefully, we will all live long, healthy, and productive lives. But it is important to keep in mind that some day we might have to rely on others to care for us.

WHAT YOU HAVE LEARNED

Complete the exercises below. When you have finished, be prepared to share your answers with your classmates.

1. Name three types of situations in which a child might need protection. Describe what you could do to help him/her.

    1.

    2.

    3.

2. Name three types of situations in which a pet might need protection. Describe what you could do to help the animal.

    1.

    2.

    3.

3. Name three types of situations in which an elderly person might need protection. Describe what you could do to help him/her.

    1.

    2.

    3.

4. Have you ever known anyone who thought about suicide? ☐ Yes ☐ No

5. Have you ever known anyone who talked about killing another human being? ☐ Yes ☐ No

If you answered "Yes" to question 4 or 5, continue with questions 6 and 7. If you answered "No" to both questions, do not go on to the next questions.

6. Have you talked with someone about either of these situations? ☐ Yes ☐ No

7. Would you feel safe talking with someone about either of these situations? ☐ Yes ☐ No
    If "Yes," who?

POTENTIALLY DESTRUCTIVE BEHAVIORS

| 24 |
Bottling Up Emotions

| 25 |
Prejudice

| 26 |
Fear

1241
BOTTLING UP EMOTIONS
(LEADER'S GUIDE)

MATERIALS NEEDED:

For each student:

- Copy of *Bottling Up Emotions* (pages 103-105)
- Pencil

LESSON:

Tell the students:

> The purpose of this lesson is to help you better understand that bottling up emotions can be detrimental to your health. Emotions that are bottled up fester and grow until they become so intense that you feel as if you are going to blow up. And that is what usually happens: You lose control.

Distribute a copy of the reproduced materials (pages 103-105) and a pencil to each student. Tell the students to read and follow the directions in *Bottling Up Emotions* and answer the questions in the *What You Have Learned* section. Set a time limit for this activity. When the allotted time is up, ask the students to share their suggestions.

Have the students put their completed papers into their notebooks to save for their own personal future reference.

BOTTLING UP EMOTIONS

How many times have you heard the phrases below? They express the feelings people have when they bottle up their emotions instead of dealing with problems as they occur. These behaviors happen when a person does not have the skills to deal with anger and solve problems or is hurt and unable to express feelings and emotions. When people are unable to say how they feel, they sometimes act out aggressively.

TIED UP IN KNOTS
What does this mean? _____
_____

BLOWING MY TOP
What does this mean? _____
_____

SEEING RED
What does this mean? _____
_____

BUTTERFLIES IN MY STOMACH
What does this mean? _____
_____

ON MY NERVES
What does this mean? _____
_____

UNDER MY SKIN
What does this mean? _____
_____

BOILING MAD
What does this mean? _____
_____

SICK TO MY STOMACH
What does this mean? _____
_____

READY TO SCREAM
What does this mean? _____
_____

When you let your emotions bottle up to the point that you are so angry that you can't think clearly, anger takes over. When this happens, you are no longer in control. You begin to think with your emotions instead of your brain—a sure recipe for trouble!

Bottling up feelings is risky.

People who bottle up or internalize their feelings are more at risk of losing control than those who express or act out their feelings. This is because they hide what's bothering them for a long time. Instead of dealing with the problem when it is small, they let it fester and build until it is much larger and less manageable than it originally was.

Quiet people often internalize their feelings. This is because speaking up does not come naturally to them. Children who are physically or sexually abused sometimes internalize feelings for fear of drawing more attention to themselves or remain quiet because they fear they are the *cause* of the abuse.

Students who bottle up their emotions often do well in school. By doing well academically, they do not have to fear having their parents come to school. Students whose parents are drug addicts, abusers, or alcoholics are embarrassed or afraid when their parents are summoned to school and do everything in their power to prevent this from happening. Many times, students who bottle up emotions are loners and are not very popular.

Talk your feelings out.

Talking things out and verbalizing feelings with responsible adults or trusted friends is the best solution. Others can often suggest ideas and say things that make you feel better. Sometimes they can even suggest ideas that hadn't occurred to you.

Students who are always in trouble at school or at home act out their problems and are easily recognized as needing help. They are referred to counselors or social workers for counseling in order to learn how to deal more effectively with their problems. Quiet children, who are troubled, are more difficult to recognize and their "hidden" problems can easily be overlooked.

Ask for help.

What can an internalizer do to get help? Asking for help is the first step. Talk with a teacher in private or with some other adult at school, at church, or in the community. Explain your problem. A teacher or other adult can refer you to a trained school social worker or counselor who will keep your conversation confidential and talk with you so you can learn healthier ways to express your emotions. You will learn to feel better about yourself and gain a sense of belonging and relief from the pain and suffering you have experienced.

WHAT YOU HAVE LEARNED

1. Why are people who bottle up their emotions more at risk of losing control than those who do not?

2. When you lose control, what are you using to think?

3. Why is talking with someone else about a problem often a good idea?

4. Whom would you talk with about a problem?

5. What is the first step that person who bottles up emotions should take to get help?

1251
PREJUDICE
(LEADER'S GUIDE)

MATERIALS NEEDED:

For each student:

- Copy of *Prejudice* (pages 107-109)
- Pencil

LESSON:

Tell the students:

> The purpose of this lesson is to help you understand how prejudice has an impact on violence. A person who is prejudiced dislikes others without even knowing them. A person who is prejudiced against a religious, racial, or ethnic group is not interested in trying to get to know anyone who is a member of that group. Prejudice, when out of hand, erupts into such violent actions as bombings, riots, and drive-by shootings. As long as prejudice is a part of our society, it will prevent communities from being safe.

Distribute a copy of the reproduced materials (pages 107-109) and a pencil to each student. Tell the students to read *Prejudice* and complete the unfinished sentences in the *What You Have Learned* section. Set a time limit for this activity. When the allotted time is up, have the students share their answers. There are no right or wrong answers, and all appropriate responses should be accepted.

Divide the students into small groups. Tell them to talk about the two situations described in the *Discussion Questions* section. When the groups have finished their discussions, ask them to share their findings with the rest of the class, either verbally or through role-play. Be sure to guide students who show signs of prejudice or lack of respect for another culture or race toward a better understanding and acceptance of others.

Have the students put their completed papers into their notebooks to save for their own personal future reference.

PREJUDICE

People who are prejudiced are unreasonable and hostile.

Prejudice is defined as unreasonable feelings, opinions, or attitudes of a hostile nature directed against a racial, religious, or national group. Two key words in the definition are *unreasonable* and *hostile. Unreasonable* is used because people who are prejudiced dislike others without taking the time to get to know them. People who are prejudiced are against a racial, national, or religious group and have unreasonable feelings of hostility. Because of this, they dislike any individual who is a member of that group. People who are prejudiced do not want or make an effort to get to know any of these people. Their prejudice often erupts into violence.

Prejudice is not directed only at racial, national, and religious groups. It also affects people who are different from most people in some way. Overweight people may be teased because of their appearance. Children can be teased because they wear braces or glasses. Physically challenged people are often avoided by others. Extremely bright children are ostracized, and children who feel sexually different are often alienated from their peers. For some reason, we want everyone to be the same as we are. Yet we say we learn from differences.

Prejudice divides communities and makes them unsafe.

At times, everyone is guilty of a prejudiced act. These acts cause pain and drive people further apart. When people are driven further apart, we lose the benefits of learning and sharing with each other. Our community also loses. When the people who live in a community do not accept one another, that community is not a safe place to live. Tensions based on prejudice erupt into groups forming gangs and into violent acts such as riots, drive-by shootings, and other illegal actions. If we are to live together peaceably, prejudice must be eradicated.

End name-calling.

We can begin by ending name-calling. Name-calling fuels anger, and anger fuels violence. There is no reason to call anyone a derogatory name, even in anger. Name-calling is only done because the name-caller is deliberately trying to hurt another human being. There are better ways to manage anger.

Reject rigidity.

Learn not to be so rigid. Rigid people have a single set of beliefs and anything that doesn't conform to those beliefs is not accepted. Rigidity can be broken down by learning to work together. Do not be afraid to accept someone who is different from you or to let someone show you a different way to do a task. Rigidity causes you to lose out on learning and sharing. When everyone is willing to work together, your home, school, community, and even our planet will be safer and better places to be.

WHAT YOU HAVE LEARNED

Complete the following statements with your thoughts about how to find solutions to end the cycle of violence based on prejudice:

1. When I see someone of another race, I feel that he/she is _____ and that makes me feel _____.

2. I wish all races of people could get along because _____
   _____.

3. I have friends who are from different racial groups, and I feel _____ about them.

4. One of the ways I can end prejudice and violence is to treat all people with ___
   _____.

5. Not calling anyone from a different racial, religious, or ethnic group a derogatory name is important because _____.

6. Name a TV show with a family or character who is racially, physically, or sexually different from yourself. _____
   Would you be this person's friend? _____.

Complete the following sentences with your ideas about how to make your world less prejudiced:

1. I can make my home less prejudiced by _____
   _____.

2. I can make my school less prejudiced by _____
   _____.

3. I can make my community less prejudiced by _____
   _____.

4. I can improve Planet Earth and the environment by _____
   _____.

DISCUSSION QUESTIONS

Work in small groups to brainstorm for answers to the following situations. Be prepared to role-play your solutions.

1. You're in a restaurant and one of the people in your group uses the "N" word to refer to African-Americans. (You may substitute another derogatory word and choose a different race or ethnic group or religion.) What do you do?

2. You and your best friend are walking down the street. An older woman sees you approaching her. She clutches her purse and moves quickly out of your way as if you were going to attack her. What do you do?

1261
FEAR
(LEADER'S GUIDE)

MATERIALS NEEDED:

For each student:

- Copy of *Fear* (pages 111-112)
- Pencil

LESSON:

Tell the students:

> The purpose of this lesson is to help you understand that fears come in many different forms and that we all fear something. Some children fear their homes, their schools, or the streets in their community. Some fear other people. Some children fear their parents dying from smoking, using drugs, or abusing alcohol. Recognizing your fears will help you become a stronger person.

Distribute a copy of the reproduced materials (pages 111-112) and a pencil to each student. Tell the students to read *Fears,* complete the *What You Have Learned* section, and answer the questions in the *Discussion Questions* section. Set a time limit for this activity. When the allotted time is up, have those students who wish to share their answers about their fears do so.

Divide the students into small groups. Tell the groups their job is to come to a common conclusion about the two *Discussion Questions.* Set a time limit for this activity. When the allotted time is up, have the groups share their decisions. Some answers may be:

1. *Police officers and military personnel should carry guns because their job is to serve and protect others.*

2. *No. Children who carry guns are afraid and feel unsafe.*

Have the students put their completed papers into their notebooks to save for their own personal future reference.

FEAR

Fear is painful.

Fear is a painful emotion. It involves terror, fright, and panic. Some children fear their homes, their schools, or the streets in their communities. Some fear other people.

Fear comes in many different forms.

Imagine a world in which a 6-year-old boy's greatest fear is being thrown from a high-rise apartment window because he refused to steal candy. Imagine a world in which a 7-year-old girl is kicked to death on a school playground by two 8-year-old boys. Imagine a world in which a child's worst nightmare is fear of being beaten, punched, and slapped by her parents. Imagine a world in which children live in homes where parents and relatives verbally and sexually abuse them. Imagine a world in which a child is afraid to sleep for fear of nightmares as a result of watching television programs filled with blood and violence. Do these incidents come from the real world or from an imaginary world?

Some children have other fears. Children who see their parents smoking fear that they might die from lung cancer. Other children, whose parents are alcoholics or drug users, fear that their parents will die from liver damage caused by excessive alcohol consumption or from drugs. Some children fear a bully at school, the walk home from school, the adult making obscene remarks on the way home, or an older brother or sister who is abusive, rather than protective. Some children might fear a parent, a teacher, or a neighbor. Other children might be afraid of a baby-sitter or of being left with relatives while a parent works. Some children are afraid of dark places and of entering dark rooms. A tragic event or illness can also cause fears.

Some students are afraid of failure and rejection. One student said he was afraid to join a gang because he feared the initiation, which involved beating him almost to death. Everyone fears something.

Fear often produces good.

Organizations like Mothers Against Drunk Drivers (MADD), AIDS Awareness Groups, and Alcoholics Anonymous were formed because of fear. Legislation like the Surgeon General's mandatory warning on cigarette packages was enacted out of the fear that one cause of lung cancer is smoking tobacco. These organizations used fear to bring about social changes without violence.

Some people carry weapons because they are afraid.

A large number of young people are carrying weapons. Do you think students who carry guns are brave and powerful, or are they just afraid? People who feel safe in their communities and schools don't need or want to carry guns.

WHAT YOU HAVE LEARNED

What are your fears? Take five minutes to think about what your fears are and to list them. Then share them, if you are comfortable doing so, with the class.

DISCUSSION QUESTIONS

Read the questions below and write your opinion about each of them. Share your opinion with your group. Your group will discuss your answer and the other group members' answers. Together, you will decide on one common answer to share with the class.

1. Who should carry guns?

   Why should these people carry guns?

2. Do you think children who carry guns feel safe?

CONSTRUCTIVE BEHAVIORS

|27|
Positive Feelings

|28|
Communicating Through Body Language

|29|
Good Manners Lead to Good Behavior

|30|
Setting Goals

|31|
Selecting and Keeping Friends

1271
POSITIVE FEELINGS
(LEADER'S GUIDE)

MATERIALS NEEDED:

For each student:

- Copy of *Positive Feelings* (pages 115-117)
- Pencil

LESSON:

Tell the students:

> The purpose of this lesson is to help you understand that feelings can be positive as well as negative. Negative feelings make you feel bad. Positive feelings, like happiness and joy, make you feel good. Your goal is to learn the meaning of 10 positive feelings by learning their definitions and associating them with something that has happened to you. It is important to talk about positive feelings, because people who can do this usually have good self-esteem. (*Leader's Note: Neglected or abused children may find it difficult to verbalize feelings.*)

Distribute a copy of the reproduced materials (pages 115-117) and a pencil to each student. Tell the students to read *Positive Feelings* and use the definitions to write the sentences in the *What You Have Learned* section. Set a time limit for this activity. When the allotted time is up, have the students share their answers to the questions. Their answers should relate to the following definitions:

1. *Excitement* is the state of being aroused or stirred up with emotions. Excitement that is the result of a happy occasion is a positive feeling.
2. *Ecstasy* is a strong feeling of joy that is the result of something really great happening to you.
3. *Joy* is a feeling of great delight or happiness.
4. *Elation* is a feeling of pride or delight.
5. *Pleasure* is a sense of enjoyment, satisfaction, or gratification.
6. *Delight* is a high degree of pleasure or enjoyment.
7. *Desire* is a longing or a craving.
8. *Enjoyment* is a feeling of pleasure or satisfaction.
9. A *thrill* is a feeling of excitement.
10. *Happiness* is the state of being glad, delighted, or pleased about a particular person, thing, or situation.

Have the students put their completed papers into their notebooks to save for their own personal future reference.

POSITIVE FEELINGS

Not all feelings are negative. Some feelings are positive, and these sensations make us feel good.

We know the meaning of negative feelings such as anger, embarrassment, sadness, and fright. But not all feelings are negative. Some feelings are positive. These are the feelings—like happiness, excitement, and delight—that make us feel good.

Negative feelings make us feel bad. Positive feelings, like happiness and joy, make us feel good.

Positive feelings make you feel good about life and about other people. They allow you to make healthy choices and decisions. If you have a positive outlook on life, you will be more likely to have the type of life you want.

When you feel good about yourself, other people will like being around you.

Positive people are the kind of people we admire and want to be like. Positive people know and like themselves and usually have a circle of friends who admire and trust them. Positive people express their feelings and communicate positive ideas and feelings to others.

When you feel good about yourself, you are better able to solve problems and resolve conflicts.

When you feel good about yourself, you know what to do when problems become more than you can handle. You know that you should seek counseling or talk with someone you trust.

People with low self-esteem don't always feel happy and don't always make good choices. They find it difficult to see the good things in life.

Being able to verbalize positive feelings about yourself is a sign of good self-esteem.

It is important to think about what positive feelings mean. You can do this by learning the meaning of words that describe these feelings. Some of these words are:

1. *Excitement* is the state of being aroused or stirred up with emotions. Excitement that is the result of a happy occasion is a positive feeling.

2. *Ecstasy* is a strong feeling of joy that is the result of something really great happening to you.

3. *Joy* is a feeling of great delight or happiness.

4. *Elation* is a feeling of pride or delight.

5. *Pleasure* is a sense of enjoyment, satisfaction, or gratification.

6. *Delight* is a high degree of pleasure or enjoyment.

7. *Desire* is a longing or a craving.

8. *Enjoyment* is a feeling of pleasure or satisfaction.

9. A *thrill* is a feeling of excitement.

10. *Happiness* is the state of being glad, delighted, or pleased about a particular person, thing, or situation.

WHAT YOU HAVE LEARNED

Directions: Positive feelings words are used every day. Refer to the definitions on the previous page. On the lines provided, write a sentence telling of a time you experienced each feeling.

1. Excitement _____
   _____

2. Ecstasy _____
   _____

3. Joy _____
   _____

4. Elation _____
   _____

5. Pleasure _____
   _____

6. Delight _____
   _____

7. Desire _____
   _____

8. Enjoyment _____
   _____

9. Thrill _____
   _____

10. Happiness _____
    _____

1281
COMMUNICATING THROUGH BODY LANGUAGE
(LEADER'S GUIDE)

MATERIALS NEEDED:

For each student:

- Copy of *Communicating Through Body Language* (pages 119-121)
- Pencil
- Construction paper, scissors, and markers or crayons (optional)

LESSON:

Tell the students:

> The purpose of this lesson is to help you understand that learning to read body language can help you resolve conflicts. Body language is nonverbal communication through facial expressions and gestures. Body language is used daily. Many facial expressions and gestures are universal. You don't have to speak in order to make them understood.

Distribute a copy of the reproduced materials (pages 119-121) and a pencil to each student. Have the students read *Communicating Through Body Language*. Set a time limit for this activity. Then have each of the students choose a partner and complete the silent communication activity in the *What You Have Learned* section. Set a time limit for this activity. When the allotted time is up, tell the students to complete their papers. When everyone has finished, have the students share their answers.

Have the students put their completed papers into their notebooks to save for their own personal future reference.

OPTIONAL ACTIVITY:

The Feelings Mask

Distribute construction paper, scissors, and markers or crayons to each student. Tell the students to choose one of the feelings drawn on the activity sheet, then draw a mask of that feeling. Tell the students not to tell anyone what feeling they are drawing. When each student has finished, cut out his/her mask. Have each student hold his/her mask in front of his/her face and have the other students guess which feeling it represents.

COMMUNICATING THROUGH BODY LANGUAGE

You can communicate without saying a word.

Have you ever had someone approach you and ask, "What's wrong?" You haven't said a word, but somehow he/she knew you were upset. The person read your body language: Your facial expression and the way you moved. Your expressions and gestures let you communicate without saying a word.

You don't have to speak in order to make body language understood.

We use body language every day. Many of the same facial expressions and gestures are used by different cultures, and you don't have to speak to make them understood. When your mouth is full and you want to say "No," you shake your head from side to side. When you want to say "Yes," you shake it up and down. When you're really mad at someone, you point and shake your finger in the person's face. When you stand with one foot shifted in front of you and your hand on your hip, it is obvious you are upset or angry. Without saying a word, you have told anyone watching you how you feel. Your body language has spoken for you.

Reading body language can help you avoid conflict.

Learning to communicate verbally is one way to resolve conflicts and prevent violence. Learning to read body language is another way to help in conflict-resolution. When you notice that another person is upset, try to stay calm by not showing your anger or fear. Staying calm and not "wearing your emotions on your sleeve" can help diffuse a situation instead of escalating it. When you are able to read body language, you will know when another person is sad, mad, or angry. Knowing this, you can choose to communicate in a helpful way or avoid the situation altogether.

WHAT YOU HAVE LEARNED

When your teacher tells you to do so, find a partner. See if you and your partner can communicate silently—through your body language—the following words or phrases. Decide which of you will go first. When the first person has finished, the second person should repeat the activity. Since your partner has the same paper you have, mix up the order of the words or phrases. Your teacher will let you know when the allotted time is up.

HELLO	**STOP**	**COME OVER HERE**
GOOD-BYE	**EXCITED**	**FEAR**
WAIT	**HAPPINESS**	**ANGER**
LOOK AT THIS	**I DON'T KNOW**	**SADNESS**

Read and answer the following questions.

1. How can you tell when your teacher is upset? _____.

2. How do you feel when your teacher is upset? _____.

3. How can you tell when your teacher is angry? _____.

4. How do you feel when your teacher is angry? _____.

5. How can you tell when your parents are upset? _____.

6. How do you feel when your parents are upset? _____.

7. How can you tell when your parents are angry? _____.

8. How do you feel when your parents are angry? _____.

9. Do your parents' and teacher's behaviors give you clues about how to act? _____.

10. Do you stay out of their way when they are angry or upset? _____.

Read the following:

Think about a time when you have had someone tell you, "I'm in a bad mood today, so don't mess with me!" A person who did not say those words may have given the same message with subtle signs, through body language.

Look at the pictures below: Label each picture with the correct feeling word.

EXCITED   HAPPY   SCARED   MAD   SAD   LONELY

1291
GOOD MANNERS LEAD TO GOOD BEHAVIOR
(LEADER'S GUIDE)

MATERIALS NEEDED:

For each student:

- Copy of *Good Manners Lead to Good Behavior* (pages 123-124)
- Pencil

LESSON:

Tell the students:

> The purpose of this lesson is to help you understand that in order to respect yourself and others, you must have a good self-image and good self-esteem. Having good manners is a sign of respect for yourself and respect for others.

Distribute a copy of the reproduced materials (pages 123-124) and a pencil to each student. Have the students read *Good Manners Lead to Good Behavior* and complete the *What You Have Learned* section. Set a time limit for this activity. When the allotted time is up, have the students share their answers with the class. The topics are subjective, and any appropriate answer should be accepted.

Have the students put their completed papers into their notebooks to save for their own personal future reference.

GOOD MANNERS LEAD TO GOOD BEHAVIOR

Treat people the way you want and expect them to treat you.

It is good manners to treat all people with dignity and respect. You cannot do this if you have little respect for yourself. Therefore, people who treat others badly probably have little self-respect. You cannot have self-respect if you do not have a good self-image and good self-esteem. This vicious cycle cannot be broken if you do not think highly of and respect yourself.

Be calm when talking with an angry person.

It is good manners to respond courteously and calmly to an angry person. Not only might it affect the way that person responds to you, but it means that you have self-control. Knowing you can control your reactions is part of having faith in yourself, which leads to self-respect.

Apologize and accept blame when you are wrong.

Having good manners includes being able to apologize and accept blame when you are wrong. Many situations that worsen could be diminished or avoided by someone apologizing or admitting the error. The way you apologize isn't important, but the fact that you apologize is very important. You can say, "I'm sorry," "I apologize," "It's my fault," "It's my mistake," or use any other words that tell the other person you realize that you were wrong and you're willing to admit it. It takes a big person to admit being wrong. The coward's way out is to blame others for his/her own mistakes.

Be respectful at home and in your community.

Having good manners means respecting others at home and in the community. Being respectful of parents is where it all starts. Talking back to and being disrespectful of parents is wrong. If you have a poor relationship with your family, being courteous can improve it. Being courteous to your family will make your life happier.

People remember when you are courteous to them. They listen to your opinions and ideas. They treat you better and like you more. Having good manners means being honest and sincere with people. People trust and admire honesty. Remember that it is important to say "Please" and "Thank you."

WHAT YOU HAVE LEARNED

AT HOME:

List at least three things you have done or said that showed good manners at home.

1. _____
2. _____
3. _____

AT SCHOOL:

List at least three things you have done or said that showed good manners at school.

1. _____
2. _____
3. _____

IN YOUR COMMUNITY:

List at least three things you have done or said that showed good manners in your community.

1. _____
2. _____
3. _____

1301
SETTING GOALS
(LEADER'S GUIDE)

MATERIALS NEEDED:

For each student:

- Copy of *Setting Goals* (pages 127-129)
- Pencil

LESSON:

Tell the students:

> The purpose of this lesson is to help you learn that goals give you a sense of purpose or objective. Setting goals helps you make good decisions. Making good decisions lets you be in control of your life, rather than letting your life be in control of you. Through goal-setting, you learn to work *with* people and not *against* them. Goal-setting helps you focus on learning to do things well.

Distribute a copy of the reproduced materials (pages 127-129) and a pencil to each student. Tell the students to read *Setting Goals,* then write a newspaper story in the *What You Have Learned* section.

Set a time limit for this activity. When the allotted time is up, have the students share their stories.

Then say:

> Look at the picture of the boy climbing the mountain. Write a goal you would like to achieve in the flag at the top of the mountain. Then starting at the bottom of the mountain, write the steps you need to take to reach your goal. Use at least five steps.

Have the students put their completed papers into their notebooks to save for their own personal future reference.

SETTING GOALS

Setting goals can make wishes a reality.

A *goal* is something to be achieved through effort. Having a goal gives you something to work toward. Do you ever say, "I should have done that," or "I would have done that if…"? Goal-setting is a mental exercise that helps you turn this type of wishful thinking into real change.

When you set goals, you are in control of making your goals a reality. Having goals helps you make better decisions. Making better decisions lets you be in control of your life, rather than letting your life be in control of you. Goal-setting also helps you deal with conflicts and control your anger.

Goal setting can teach you to work with people, not against them.

Goal-setting can help you turn people who act like enemies into friends. You can do this if your goal is to make caring comments and not say mean things that hurt others. When you hear others say mean, nasty things, you need to remember that these are people who hurt inside and who think they feel better when they hurt others. Sometimes you may even want to say things to hurt others before they hurt you. But remember: When you do this, then you are acting like they do and you hurt inside as much as they do.

A goal could be to say something nice to someone every day or to change a negative fact into a positive one. For example, if Jackie has broken eyeglasses, don't focus on that. Find something good about Jackie, such as having nice hair. Comment on her nice hair, not on the broken eyeglasses. Try this approach and see how differently people react to you.

Goal-setting helps you focus on learning to do things well.

You may have several internal conflicts. Internal conflicts are arguments you have with yourself or, possibly, worries about something that you don't feel you can influence in any way. You may be overweight, have difficulty completing homework, or not be big enough to make the football team. Whatever your internal conflicts may be, you will perform better in and out of school when you learn to control them. Goal-setting can help you do this. Setting a goal to cut down on the fatty foods, do homework as soon as you get home, or do weight-training might be solutions that you can reach through setting a goal.

Goal-setting benefits everyone.

When you set goals, you do more than improve yourself. You also help others. Your parents or teachers may not bother you as much, or you may find that you have more friends. One goal you might set that will benefit others is to do or say something good for someone else every day. One goal you might set that will benefit yourself is to pick one thing that is blocking you from achieving something you want. Devise a step-by-step plan to work toward your goal every day until you have achieved what you want.

WHAT YOU HAVE LEARNED

ME IN THE FUTURE!

Write a newspaper story about something you would like your friends to read about you in the future.

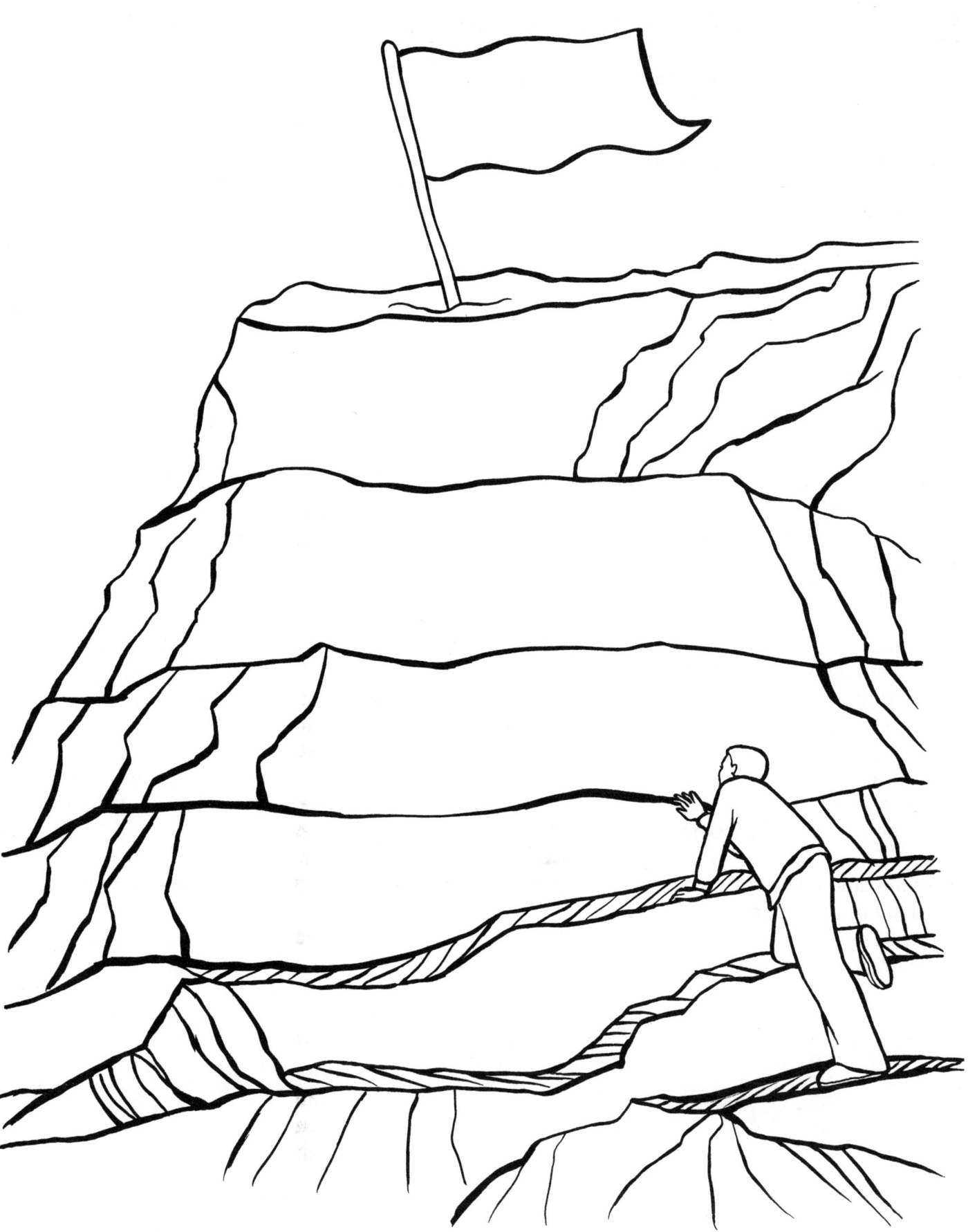

SELECTING AND KEEPING FRIENDS
(LEADER'S GUIDE)

MATERIALS NEEDED:

For each student:

- Copy of *Selecting and Keeping Friends* (pages 131-133)
- Pencil

LESSON:

Tell the students:

> The purpose of this lesson is to help you understand how to select and keep friends. *Friends* are people who are supportive, encourage you to do your best, enjoy common interests, and share secrets. Sometimes friends disagree and argue. Sometimes they feel jealous. This is a natural part of any friendship. Friends may disagree, but they never try to hurt each other or put one another in danger.

Distribute a copy of the reproduced materials (pages 131-133) and a pencil to each student. Tell the students to read *Selecting and Keeping Friends,* then complete the *What You Have Learned* section. Set a time limit for this activity. When the allotted time is up, ask the students to share what they learned about their friendships.

Divide the students into small groups. Tell them to discuss the tips for acting positively with friends found in the *Selecting and Keeping Friends* text. Set a time limit for this activity. When everyone has finished, ask the groups to share their findings.

Have the students put their completed papers into their notebooks to save for their own personal future reference.

SELECTING AND KEEPING FRIENDS

What is a friend?

A *friend* is a person who knows and likes someone. A friend is a companion, a well-wisher, and a confidant. Your friends are the people who know you better than anybody and who are always there for you.

What is friendship?

Friendship is a relationship between friends. It is a kindly feeling or disposition.

Knowing how to select and keep friends is an important skill.

Friends are people who are supportive. They encourage each other to do their best, enjoy common interests, and share secrets. They feel comfortable with each other and are willing to protect each other and keep each other safe.

Sometimes friends disagree and argue. Sometimes friends feel a little rivalry and jealousy. This is a natural part of friendship, as of any relationship. Friends may disagree, but they never try to hurt each other or put one another in danger. Friends may get jealous of one another. But when they see jealousy interfering with their friendship, they talk the problem out and put an end to it.

TIPS FOR ACTING POSITIVELY WITH FRIENDS

Why do some people have friends while others have none?

1. People who have friends act in a positive manner.

People who have friends know how to act in a positive way with their peers. They know how to cooperate, be helpful, show interest, and pay compliments.

2. People who have friends cooperate.

A cooperative person knows how to take turns, share toys and games, and will leave without being upset if the other person says he/she doesn't feel like playing. A cooperative person knows how to work with other people.

3. People who have friends are helpful.

Helpful people offer to help others in work or play. They volunteer to get, bring, or carry things for others without having to be asked. They offer to console someone who is in pain. They don't get angry when others don't help them.

4. People who have friends show interest in what others are doing.

People who have friends show interest in others by being cheerful, smiling appropriately, and maintaining good eye contact. They show interest in what others are doing by asking questions and listening to the way that others answer. They share and keep secrets. They offer positive solutions to other people's problems.

5. People who have friends know how to express affection.

People who have friends know how to express affection by doing things like paying compliments to friends. They are able to hug and touch others and let their friends know that they like them. People who have friends are not clingy, possessive, or jealous.

WHAT HAVE YOU LEARNED

Directions: Think about your friends. How do they stack up? Put a check (✓) in the box for the correct response.

	YES	NO
1. Would a friend ask another friend to take drugs?	☐	☐
2. Do your friends ask you to do things you know are legally or morally wrong?	☐	☐
3. Do your friends tell lies about you or try to get you into trouble?	☐	☐
4. Do your friends talk about you behind your back?	☐	☐
5. If your mom set a 9:00 curfew, would your friends try to get you to break it?	☐	☐
6. Do your friends make fun of other people and encourage you to do the same?	☐	☐
7. Do your friends talk badly about their parents, or yours, behind their backs?	☐	☐
8. Are your friends starting to talk positively about gangs and/or weapons?	☐	☐

If you had more than five "Yes" answers, it's time to reevaluate your friendships. You may need to start thinking about making some new friends. First, try talking with your friends to see if you can get them to see your way of thinking. If you can't, and they're real friends, don't give up. Try to help them or suggest getting help for them. If the situation is still unchanged, you have to make a decision. You have to decide how long to hang in. You don't want to become vulnerable and get sucked into negative behavior just to be a friend.

SELF-AWARENESS

|32|
Self-Esteem

|33|
I Need to Improve

|34|
Good Self-Esteem Makes You Feel Good

|35|
I Am a Strong Person

1321
SELF-ESTEEM
(LEADER'S GUIDE)

MATERIALS NEEDED:

For each student:

- Copy of *Self-Esteem* (pages 137-139)
- Pencil
- Large piece of drawing paper (optional)

LESSON:

Tell the students:

The purpose of this lesson is to help you understand that self-esteem is the foundation of your personality. It determines your ability to make good decisions about your actions with friends, in your community, and at home and school. People with low self-esteem are not always good decision-makers. These people should not feel as if things can never change for them, because self-esteem is a learned behavior. It *can* be changed.

The first step is knowing what your strengths and weaknesses are. Then surround yourself with positive people who eliminate negative behavior and peer pressure. This will also improve your interpersonal relationships and result in better self-esteem.

Distribute a copy of the reproduced materials (pages 137-139) to each student. Have the students read *Self-Esteem,* then complete the *What You Have Learned* section. Set a time limit for this activity. When the allotted time is up, have the students discuss their answers. The questions are subjective, and all appropriate answers should be accepted.

Have the students put their completed papers into their notebooks to save for their own personal future reference.

OPTIONAL ACTIVITY:

Distribute a large piece of drawing paper and a pencil to each student. Tell the students to draw an outline figure nearly as large as the drawing paper. Review the meaning of *self-concept*. Then tell the students to fill in the outline by writing about their own self-concept.

SELF-ESTEEM

Self-esteem is defined as respect for or a favorable impression of one's self—you!

Self-esteem is a term used to describe your feelings about yourself. When you feel good about yourself, you have high self-esteem. When you don't like yourself very much, you have low self-esteem.

Self-concept shapes self-esteem.

Self-concept is how you see yourself and how you feel about yourself. It is how secure, confident, and competent you view yourself as being. Self-concept shapes a person and is the way you judge yourself. These judgments shape and mold your self-esteem.

Having high self-esteem is important.

People with high self-esteem feel good about themselves. They feel they are able to make good decisions. They can say "No" when someone approaches them about joining a gang, using drugs, or doing something else that they feel or know is morally wrong. People with good self-esteem are able to stand up for themselves and make good decisions based on the choices they have.

Low self-esteem can give you an untrue picture of yourself.

People with low self-esteem often tell lies and describe their families as being very different from what they are. People with low self-esteem find it hard to accurately describe their friends, family, and home because to do so is painful for them. People with low self-esteem who live in poor conditions and who are talking with someone who doesn't know where they live may describe their home as very luxurious, or at least middle-class and comfortable. They may describe their parents as being professional people like doctors, nurses, or teachers because they are afraid of how the other person might view them if he/she knew them as they really are. People who are unable to talk about their lives in terms of reality hurt inside and feel empty. They believe that in order to survive, they need to create—even if it is unreal—a nicer, safer world for themselves.

People with low self-esteem don't always make good decisions.

People with low self-esteem are often followers who are easily influenced by others. They are often taken advantage of and persuaded to do wrong.

Low self-esteem can be changed to high self-esteem.

First, it is necessary to assess where you are and to know who you are. This will help you know what your strengths and weaknesses are. You must recognize that self-esteem is a learned behavior and that teachers, counselors, and parents can teach you to improve your self-esteem, much as they might teach you math. For example, if you are overweight, you can learn to like yourself the way you are. Or, if you want, you can lose weight. If you are short and being short bothers you, you need to learn to accept yourself as you are, because you certainly can't stretch yourself. Even though adults, like teachers and counselors, can teach you ways to change your self-esteem, it is *you* who must learn to like yourself. *You* are the person with the power. *You* must believe in yourself and not blame others for things that happen to you.

You can change your self-esteem by:

1. changing your way of thinking and by thinking positive thoughts.
2. telling yourself, "I am somebody," and believing you are special.
3. finding a mentor (a wise and trusted person).
4. being friendly and positive.
5. starting to look for friends and peers who will be positive role models.
6. surrounding yourself with positive people.
7. taking care of yourself physically as well as mentally.

Positive people influence your self-esteem.

Surrounding yourself with positive people eliminates negative behavior and peer pressure. These people will improve your interpersonal relationships, and improving these relationships helps you develop healthier self-esteem. Having people around who are making successes of themselves is a healthy way of improving your own self-esteem.

It is necessary to take care of yourself both mentally and physically.

Taking care of yourself includes proper diet and nutrition, relaxation, and exercise. If you are overweight, you can take charge of your life by dieting and exercising. If you are uptight and tense, you can take charge of yourself by learning ways to relax. If you are a finicky or poor eater, you can take charge of yourself by improving your diet. The sooner you start taking charge of your life, the happier you will be.

Don't expect miracles.

Your self-esteem will not change overnight. The change will be gradual. Your behaviors were established over a long period of time, so expect it to take time to change them. Be satisfied with and aware of each step forward and keep going!

WHAT YOU HAVE LEARNED

Name five positive things about yourself.

1. _____
2. _____
3. _____
4. _____
5. _____

Name the three most important people in your life.

1. _____
2. _____
3. _____

The Real Me

1. My hair is _____.
2. I'm as tall as _____.
3. If I were an animal, I'd be a _____.
4. The silliest thing I do is _____.
5. When I get real angry, I _____.
6. Sometimes I get mad when _____.
7. The thing that makes me cry is _____.
8. When I feel lonely, I _____.
9. I feel sad when I think of _____.
10. The last time I cried, I felt _____.
11. I get discouraged when I _____.
12. I give up after _____.
13. When I think about dying, I _____.
14. The easiest thing for me to do is _____.
15. The hardest thing for me to do is _____.
16. My greatest strength is _____.
17. My weakness is _____.
18. The world problem I would like to solve is _____.

1331
I NEED TO IMPROVE
(LEADER'S GUIDE)

MATERIALS NEEDED:

For each student:

- Copy of *I Need to Improve* (page 141)
- Pencil

LESSON:

Tell the students:

> The purpose of this lesson is to help you understand your weaknesses. In order to improve and grow, you must be able to identify your own weaknesses and work toward improving them. You will receive a questionnaire. Answer it as honestly as you can. When you are finished, we will discuss the answers, and our discussion may give you a better idea of what you need to do in order to overcome your weaknesses.

Distribute a copy of the reproduced material (page 141) to each student. Tell the students to complete the sentences. When the allotted time is up, encourage all the students to share their answers, but do not to force an unwilling student to participate. Since the questions are subjective, the answers will vary. Accept all appropriate answers.

Have the students put their completed papers into their notebooks to save for their own personal future reference.

I NEED TO IMPROVE

1. I get into trouble at home because I _____
   _____.

2. I get into trouble at school because I _____
   _____.

3. I get into trouble when I don't listen because I _____
   _____.

4. When I come to school mad, I get into trouble because_____
   _____.

5. I would not have had a bad day if I had _____
   _____.

6. When I go home mad, I get into trouble because I _____
   _____.

7. If I had not become mad, I _____
   _____.

8. What gets me into trouble with my brother(s) or sister(s) is _____
   _____.

9. The thing I am most frightened or afraid of is _____
   _____.

10. When other people do things differently than I do, it makes me feel _____
    _____.

11. The person I am the most afraid of is _____
    _____.

12. The things I want to know more about are _____
    _____.

13. When I wake up, I think about coming to school and _____
    _____.

1341
GOOD SELF-ESTEEM MAKES YOU FEEL GOOD
(LEADER'S GUIDE)

MATERIALS NEEDED:

For each student:

- Copy of *Good Self-Esteem Makes You Feel Good* (pages 143-144)
- Pencil

LESSON:

Tell the students:

> The purpose of this lesson is to help you understand that *self-esteem* is a term used to describe how you feel about yourself. *Self-concept* is a term used to describe how secure, confident, and competent you consider yourself.

Distribute the reproduced materials (pages 143-144) and a pencil to each student. Tell the students to read *Good Self-Esteem Makes You Feel Good,* then complete the *What You Have Learned* section. Set a time limit for this activity. When the allotted time is up, have the students share their answers. The questions are subjective, and all appropriate answers should be accepted.

Have the students put their completed papers into their notebooks to save for their own personal future reference.

GOOD SELF-ESTEEM MAKES YOU FEEL GOOD

Thinking positively about yourself is essential for good self-esteem.

You have good self-esteem when you:

- feel secure and safe, because you trust the people around you.
- achieve a feeling of success.
- feel competent because you are surrounded by supportive people who instill their knowledge and share their experiences with you at home, at school, and in the community.
- are encouraged to try new ideas without fear of ridicule if you fail.
- have a sense of belonging and connectedness in your home, at school, and in your community.
- set goals and work to attain them.
- have a sense of purpose and responsibility.
- know who you are inside and out and feel good about yourself.

If you think you're going to do well, you have a better chance of doing well. If you think negatively and think you're going to fail or do poorly, you have a better chance of failing or doing poorly. Learning to think positively about yourself is an important part of improving your self-esteem.

WHAT YOU HAVE LEARNED

Answer the questions below by putting a check (✓) in one of the three boxes.

	Always	Sometimes	Hardly Ever
1. I believe in myself.	☐	☐	☐
2. I believe I make good choices and decisions.	☐	☐	☐
3. I can talk about my problems.	☐	☐	☐
4. I feel that others like me.	☐	☐	☐
6. I feel that I look good.	☐	☐	☐
7. I am a good listener.	☐	☐	☐
8. I can take criticism.	☐	☐	☐
9. I am an independent person.	☐	☐	☐
10. I don't give up easily.	☐	☐	☐
11. I am an organized person.	☐	☐	☐
12. I am a good sport.	☐	☐	☐
13. I don't always have to win to enjoy a game.	☐	☐	☐
14. I get along well with my family.	☐	☐	☐
15. I have good friends.	☐	☐	☐

Complete the following sentences by filling in the blanks with words that best describe you.

1. My hair is _____(color) and it is _____ (curly, straight, wavy, short, long). I weigh _____ (pounds), and I am _____ feet _____ inches (tall).

2. In school, I am good at _____(subject), but not as good at _____(subject).

3. I seldom get bored, because I like to _____ .
   I always find something to do with my time, like _____ .

4. Next year, I want to learn more about _____
   to help myself improve _____ .

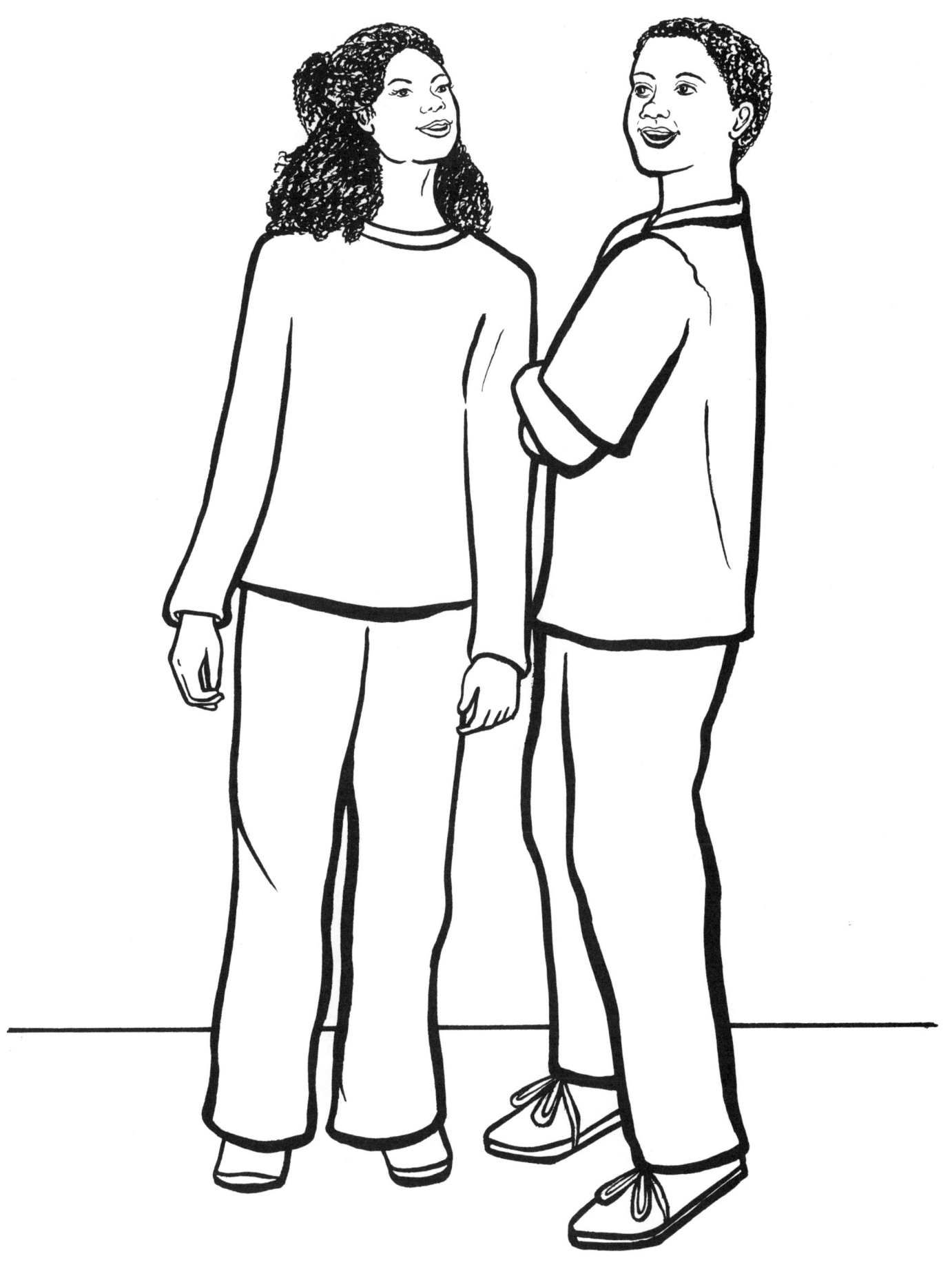

1351
I AM A STRONG PERSON
(LEADER'S GUIDE)

MATERIALS NEEDED:

For each student:

- Copy of *I Am a Strong Person* (page 147)
- Pencil

LESSON:

Tell the students:

> The purpose of this lesson is to help you understand and be aware of your strengths and of how you help others around you. This lesson will also help you recognize the people in your life who have helped shape and mold you into the person you are today.

Distribute a copy of the reproduced material (page 147) to each student. Tell the students to complete the unfinished sentences. Set a time limit for this activity. When the allotted time is up, have the students share their answers. Encourage all students to share their answers, but do not force an unwilling student to participate. The questions are open-ended and subjective, so the answers will vary. Accept all appropriate answers.

Have the students put their completed papers into their notebooks to save for their own personal future reference.

I AM A STRONG PERSON

1. My best subject in school is _____ because _____
   _____.

2. I help my best friends by _____
   _____.

3. When I see someone teasing or hurting someone, I _____
   _____.

4. I plan to learn more about _____
   _____.

5. I'm proud of myself because I helped my parent (or guardian) _____
   _____.

6. What is good about me is _____
   _____.

7. My parents make me feel good when they _____
   _____.

8. My brother(s) and sister(s) make me feel good when they _____
   _____.

9. The person who helps me learn is _____.

10. The things I like best about school are _____
    _____.

GLOSSARY

GLOSSARY

Anger	An upset feeling that occurs when something appears to be unfair or when you feel threatened or in danger
Assault	A deliberate act that puts another person in fear of immediate physical harm. No physical contact is required in committing an assault.
Boredom	What you feel when you are not interested in something or are tired of it
Burglary	When an unauthorized person enters a vehicle or structure with the intent of taking property (In a burglary, the property is taken from the vehicle or structure. In a robbery, it is taken from the person.)
Child Abuse	Harm inflicted on children by adults
Conflict	A disagreement, quarrel, or controversy
Crime	Any serious violation of a society's laws
Delight	A high degree of pleasure or enjoyment
Depression	What you feel when you are in a bad situation and cannot see any way out
Desire	A longing or a craving
Disappointment	What you feel when someone breaks a promise or fails you in some other way or when things don't happen the way you hoped they would
Domestic Violence	A violent act that occurs when family members fight and try to hurt each other
Elation	A feeling of pride or delight
Embarrassment	What you feel when someone makes fun of you or ridicules you
Enjoyment	A feeling of pleasure or satisfaction
Excitement	What you feel when you become agitated or stirred up
Ecstasy	A strong feeling of joy
External Conflict	Conflict with another person or between groups or nations
Fear	A powerful sensation of fright, panic, and terror.
Frustration	What you feel when something that you have planned is changed by someone else or when you are trying to do something and are unable to accomplish it
Goal	The result or achievement toward which effort is directed
Happiness	The state of being glad, delighted, or pleased about a particular person, thing, or situation

Homicide	The deliberate killing of one human being by another
Hurt Feelings	A sense of distress that occurs when someone makes fun of you or ridicules you
Hate Violence	Hate crimes against members of ethnic groups (racial violence) or religious denominations, people whose sexual orientation is different from one's own, or those who have physical or mental disabilities
Internal Conflict	A struggle with one's self
Joy	A feeling of great delight or happiness
Juvenile	A young person, generally under 18 years of age
Juvenile Court	A court of law having jurisdiction over minors. *Minors* generally refers to those under 18 years of age
Juvenile Crime	A serious wrongdoing committed by a young person
Juvenile Delinquency	Any illegal or antisocial behavior on the part of a minor
Mentor	A wise and trusted person
Modeling	An imitation or copying of another's actions
Murder	The unlawful killing of a human being with malice aforethought
Pleasure	A sense of enjoyment, satisfaction, or gratification
Prejudice	Unreasonable feelings, opinions, or attitudes of a hostile nature directed against a racial, religious, or national group
Robbery	A felonious taking of something of value from another person or from his/her immediate control by force or threatened force
Sadness	What you feel when you lose something or someone close to you
Scare	To cause a feeling of being threatened or in danger
Self-Esteem	Respect for or a favorable impression of one's self
Stalking	The tracking/pursuit of game animals or other victims
Self-Control	Being in charge of yourself and having the ability to control your feelings, thoughts, and actions
Sexual Violence	A physical act of aggression or force or a threat which involves the touching of another's intimate parts, or forcing a person to touch another person's intimate parts
Suicide	The act of deliberately taking one's own life
Thrill	A sudden strong feeling of excitement
Violence	A rough or injurious physical force or power

OTHER MAR*CO MATERIALS BY CAMMIE MCDANIEL

Situational Problem-Solving
(Problem-Solving Situations for Middle/Junior and High School)